Tangible

REVEALING GOD'S DESIRE TO REVEAL HIMSELF

Tangible

REVEALING GOD'S DESIRE TO REVEAL HIMSELF

Joseph Cook

TATE PUBLISHING
AND ENTERPRISES, LLC

Tangible
Copyright © 2014 by Joseph Cook. All rights reserved.

No part of this publication may be reproduced, stored in a retrieval system or transmitted in any way by any means, electronic, mechanical, photocopy, recording or otherwise without the prior permission of the author except as provided by USA copyright law.

The opinions expressed by the author are not necessarily those of Tate Publishing, LLC.

Published by Tate Publishing & Enterprises, LLC
127 E. Trade Center Terrace | Mustang, Oklahoma 73064 USA
1.888.361.9473 | www.tatepublishing.com

Tate Publishing is committed to excellence in the publishing industry. The company reflects the philosophy established by the founders, based on Psalm 68:11,
"The Lord gave the word and great was the company of those who published it."

Book design copyright © 2014 by Tate Publishing, LLC. All rights reserved.
Cover design by Caleb Pena

Published in the United States of America

ISBN: 978-1-63449-491-5
1. Religion/ Christian Life/ Spiritual Growth
2. Religion/ Christian Life/ Personal Growth
14.09.17

To my wife, Kim. You are such a light for me. Thank you for always supporting and encouraging me. I love sharing life with you.

Acknowledgements

I want to thank the following people:

My parents- Linda Malcom and Stephen Cook
My family
Kim Cook
Nathan and Katelyn Boyd
Cameron Smith
Dara "Doc" Wakefield
Caleb Pena
The pastors of Connect City Church
Walton County Christian Learning Center

To all of those who have mentored me, coached me, and loved me, this book would not have existed without your influence.

I also want to thank Tate Publishing for making this book available in print.

Finally, I want to thank Jesus for taking my place on the cross. His love was my guiding light for every word. Because of His grace, I am redeemed for God's glory.

Table of Contents

Introduction	11
Nice to Meet You	17
Good Teacher	35
Competitive-Natured	55
A Little More Conversation	77
Open the Blinds	94
Gone Fishing	116
Do You Believe in Miracles?	142
The Hill in the Race	163
The Simple Equation	192
Lose Yourself	212
The Power Within	231
The Way	256
Conclusion	288

Introduction

The Brown Paper Bag

I do not particularly enjoy meeting someone for the first time. I actually find it to be tremendously awkward in most cases. This is interesting because the most valuable part of my life is the relationships I have with other people. It just so happens that the only way to establish a relationship with someone comes through the gauntlet of getting to know that person.

It is tough getting to know someone you do not know yet. After all, you don't know them. You don't know if you can trust them. You don't know if they have the same sense of humor as you. You don't know what they enjoy doing. Most importantly, you don't even know if they want to know you. Rejection, loneliness, and sometimes enemies are born when this process goes down hill, and this can be quite costly. However, the value I find in a good relationship far exceeds the costs of a bad one. This makes the risk worth taking every time. If only there was an easier way to get to know people.

When I was in school, the most awkward moments were within the first week of classes. This is because no one was exposing his or her true identity yet. With some exceptions, no one knew anyone else, so it was difficult to open yourself up. Luckily, I had some great teachers who made this process much easier. They came up with games called "icebreakers." These games were a camouflaged way of helping us to break down our walls and get to know each other.

My favorite icebreaker game involved a brown paper bag. The teacher gave each student a brown paper bag and instructed us to go home and fill it with 10 items. Those items had to define who you were. Here are some items that would be in my brown paper bag today. One item would be a cross necklace to represent my faith. I would put in my wedding ring to symbolize my love for my wife. There would be a baseball to show my passion for sports. Another item would be a hook to reveal how much I enjoy fishing. I think you get the idea.

There is a reason this icebreaker is much more than a show-and-tell game. My faith, my love, my passion, and my enjoyment all have one thing in common. They are intangible. You cannot see, hear, or touch any of these traits, but they are all real nonetheless. Although these characteristics are completely invisible, they are revealed in visible ways. Through each tangible object in that brown paper bag, every part of who I am is fully exposed for the world to see.

One of the greatest tragedies in life is failing to notice the very thing we were created to see. God is not tangible. This is the very reason so many people give to explain their disbelief. What if the key to finding an invisible God was taking a deeper look at what is already seen? For all of us, it is clear that God is invisible. Scripture actually tells us in 1 John 4:12 that no one has ever seen God. This may be why it is so hard for us to believe in or connect with God. But what if there *was* a way to see Him?

The goal of this book is to reveal that God has a brown paper bag of His own. What if everything God created, including you and me, had a purpose in exposing who He is? There are tangible objects all around us. This book, the chair you're sitting in, and the people around you are all tangible objects. We have always believed they have a specific purpose, but what if that purpose was bigger than we ever thought? What if their purpose was to make an invisible God more visible and an intangible God more tangible?

I am not saying that the Creator is in every creation or is a specific creation. I am proclaiming that the Creator can be revealed *through* His creation. For instance, God is not a tree, but part of His character can be revealed through a tree. I am not a baseball. The ball in my bag simply displayed a portion of my character. The same can be done for God.

What if audibly hearing God speak came through an audible conversation with someone else? What if visibly seeing God's creativity came through finding a flower-painted meadow? How different would your life be if you could see God in everything you experience? The goal of this book is to open our eyes to the reality of God all around us. Seeing the Creator differently may come through seeing His creations differently. Just like the characteristics found in my bag, God's love, compassion, mercy, justice, and grace are completely invisible. When these invisible characteristics are revealed in visible ways, our intangible God becomes more real and more tangible.

As possible as it is to actually see God moving in real ways, this is not what drives our relationship with Him. The difference maker in the life of any follower is faith. Paul tells us in 2 Corinthians 5:7, "We live by faith and not by sight." Hebrews 11:1 adds to this idea by explaining that faith is confidence in what we hope for and assurance about what we do not see. While the goal of this book is to open our eyes to the reality of God all around us, faith is more important than sight. Most of us may think that *seeing* God strengthens our faith, but it is actually our faith that directs our vision. As followers, we will never be able to see God in a real way without faith. As we seek God together on this journey, ask Him to purify your heart, which will ignite your faith.

> *"Blessed are the pure in heart, for they shall see God."*
> Matthew 5:8 (English Standard Version)

Chapter 1

Nice to Meet You
It may take an introduction to see God.

Bedtime stories are extremely magical when you are a child. It's hard to say what exactly makes them so magical, but they are nonetheless. Most children will say they love the adventure, action, romance, or maybe the idea of the possibility of one day becoming one of the valiant characters depicted by their creative parents. Other children might just want a distraction or something to think about to guide them to sleep so they do not have to worry about what is lurking around in the darkness of their slightly cracked-open closet; it may also be plausible that they are just cherishing those last few moments of the day with their mom and dad. Parents are more likely to enjoy giving the stories because they usually work better than drugging the child with a Benadryl to finally get them to sleep. What ever the reason may be, there is something incredible that happens during this time of bonding between a child and their parents.

I was one of those children when I was growing up. I have an older brother and sister along with a younger sister, and our mother would read us a story every night before we went to bed. These stories were filled with brave men and soldiers, princesses being saved by their heroes, talking animals, mysterious lands, and impossible feats like the earth being gulfed up completely by water. I was in awe every time my mother would rock my little boy world with another new adventure. I went to bed dreaming I would hopefully become one of the courageous warriors I had learned about each night. As I grew, I eventually came to the conclusion that there was such a thing as make-believe. I found out that not all movies were true and that there are tons of stories that people make up simply for entertainment. This new revelation was troubling to me as a youngster because I wanted to become the kind of man I heard stories about, and if all the stories were imaginary, I knew this would be impossible.

I reached the age where I was old enough to go to children's church and attend vacation Bible school. I did not like being separated from my parents, but I remember going and hearing the same stories that my mother would tell me before I would go to bed. I was flabbergasted by the thought that they knew the same stories but thought they must have talked to my mother to know what stories I enjoyed. I began asking questions about these stories and pondered if the Sunday school teacher had borrowed the same book from our house. I was eventually informed that the stories were true. Everything I had been told was true; the adventures, the action, the killing, the saving, etc. What was even better was that all these stories could easily be found in a book called the Bible.

THE MYSTERIOUS AUTHOR

I soon reached the age where I understood the concept that if there is a story or a book, there must be someone who wrote the book or created the story. I then found out all of these stories I fell in love with were all written by the same author, and I wanted to know who that was. I was told that this author's name was God. He did not have a last name or middle name; He just went by God. I wanted to know about God, so I asked even more questions about who God was. I asked about how He came up with these amazing stories and found that He not only wrote these true stories, but He created the entire universe! This God guy sounded pretty cool.

Anyone who claims to have grown up in a Christian home or grew up going to church would have a similar experience to the one I just described. We grew up going to Bible school or children's church and were told about who God was and what He did through these unbelievable stories. We had the knowledge of God down pat and could probably tell you more about Him than most adults today could tell you. The only problem is that knowledge became the only thing we were filled with. I remember being told at vacation Bible school about how to become saved. Romans 10:9 states that if you confess with your mouth and believe in your heart that Jesus is Lord and God raised Him from the dead you will be saved. I remember thinking that was quite simple, and I had learned about hell by this point and knew I definitely did not want to go there. I decided being saved and being able to go to heaven was the better option, so I knew I just had to say, "Jesus is Lord," and believe the stories I had been told. I would then be able to get into Heaven Land where I could have anything I wanted exactly when I wanted it! Who wouldn't want that? That was the extent of my faith. Since I believed that

God was real, I would go to heaven. Nothing changed. I believed that there was a God, but I also strongly believed in Santa Claus as a child (I'm sorry if I just ruined that for you). God was still invisible, and I had no recollection of ever hearing or seeing Him. God was like a million dollars for me. I believed it was real and knew the lucky people in life had it, but I had never seen a million dollars. Few people have. A million dollars certainly existed, but it was not tangible for me.

I remember going camping with my father a lot as a child. One spring, we went camping at this state park in north Georgia, and my dad allowed me to invite one of my best friends whose name was Josh. We got to the campground and finding our goal for the week did not take long. As soon as we pulled in and set everything up, Josh and I caught glimpse of two teenaged females that looked to be around our age. We chased them around all week trying to gather up enough courage to actually talk to them instead of our manly attempts of impressing them with our monkey bar skills. The night before we were about to go make our move, I remember having this one conversation with Josh that changed everything for me. We were walking around the campground, and I remember him saying, "Joseph, I feel like God's telling me we should not try to go and talk to those girls." I did not really react, but I thought he was coo-coo for cocoa puffs; first, because I really wanted to talk to the girls, and secondly, because he thought God, the creator of the universe, had given him this instruction. I had never heard God tell me anything. What did He sound like? Did I miss something? I already confessed that Jesus was Lord; I believed in God. When was I supposed to have a conversation with Him? I felt like I had missed a meeting with my boss that I was unaware of. This was a crazy thought for me because God had never been tangible in my life. He was never someone I could see or hear or talk to. I knew who God was, but I didn't think He could know me. We had never met, and if we did, I did not remember the introduction. I never got to shake His hand and say, "It's nice to meet you." I never had an encounter with God.

THE CRUCIAL ENCOUNTER

Every single relationship begins with one thing, an encounter. It is impossible to say you know someone or have a relationship with someone if you have never had an encounter with them or if there has never been an introduction.

My buddy, Cameron, is one of my best friends. The first time Cameron and I met was with a group of mutual friends. We all went to a corn maze and then went to spend the night at one of the girl's parents' cabin in the Blue Ridge Mountains. There were several of us with not as many places to sleep, so you can see where this is going. I had never met this guy, and now I have to share a bed with him? Don't worry; this is not going to get awkward. Just before we went to bed with the great pillow-wall divider, we shook hands and said, "Nice to meet you." It was a little strange, but we got over it and slept fully clothed after some manly pillow talk, if there is such a thing. He is one of my best friends today and one of the guys I will go to about anything. In the cabin is where it all started. This friendship is only possible because there was a meeting. We had now met and were able to get to know each other. There was an encounter and an introduction, and a pretty unique one at that.

I will share another example. There is a special woman in my life whose name is Kim. We are newly married, and I could not be more blessed. I remember the night we met like it was yesterday. It was actually a few years ago, and we were attending the same church as college students in

Rome, Georgia. I remember seeing her for the first time as I blurred everything else out. Guys, you know what I'm talking about. Everything goes still; no sound, no one moving, time stops, and there is only her for this brief moment. It was the first sighting. I knew that I had to get to know her; I wanted to know who she was, what she liked, what her name was and everything else you can possibly know about someone. Although I had made eye contact and she was now existed to me, there was no relationship. I knew she was there, but I did not know her. I had not met her. There was no introduction. It was not until a couple weeks later that I gained the courage and boldness to actually go up to her and introduce myself. I was so nervous with sweaty hands and stomach turning, but I made my move. She was volunteering at our church coffee shop, and I was getting ready to lead my high school small group. I went up to her and introduced myself trying to show my backbone. The meeting was mutual as she also introduced herself, and the conversations began. Two years later, I sit here feeling so blessed to have someone like Kim in my life. I am in love with her, and this could not have been possible without the first introduction. No relationship started until I actually went up and spoke to her. I did not know her before that encounter, and she could not have possibly known me. Every relationship has a tangible introduction.

MEETING GOD

Going back to my teenage years, I remember thinking that I had never been introduced to this God. I was told about who He was and what He was like, but I had never met Him. He was not tangible to me. He was an invisible, silent, and hidden God. Fortunately, this all changed when I attended my first youth conference. It was called Acquire the Fire, and I had no idea what to expect. We had about 15 kids in our group with more middle than high school students. The conference was a weekend-long event, but it only took the first night to change my life. We arrived to the arena the Friday night, and I was completely unaware of what was about to go down. Worship began as the arena was filling with thousands of students lifting up their voices. I was never comfortable singing in church, and if you have a voice like mine, you understand why. There were enough voices to drown me out, so I thought I was in the clear to participate. Before I could open my mouth and join in, I paused and observed what was happening in the arena. I had never witnessed such an event. I stood silent with eyes open as I turned my head 360 degrees to observe. Every student was standing with their eyes closed and their arms lifted as high as they could reach as if they were waiting for someone to pull them up to the sky. I was in awe. These teenagers were not merely yelling some lyrics from a favorite song, but it was as if they were speaking to someone and confessing their love for whomever it was they were talking to. I had enough common sense to know who they were singing to, but I still could not understand it. They were having a conversation with God through song, and from what I observed this was not a one-sided conversation. They knew Him. You could see the relationship clearly in the way they were worshiping. It was as if they could see God, and the way they were singing to Him revealed their knowledge of Him actually listening to them. It was remarkable, and I wanted what they had. I wanted to be able to know this God I had been told about. I wanted to actually have a conversation with the God my mother had told me bedtime stories about. I wanted to be able to talk to Him for the first time. I wanted Him to know me and know that I existed. All I needed was the chance to introduce myself.

At the end of the message that night, the speaker arranged the meeting. He asked that if there was anyone who wanted to meet God for the first time and get to know Him to come down to the alter where the cross was standing tall. This was it! This was my opportunity to meet the God of the bible, the creator, and the author. I ran down the arena steps with hundreds of others toward the cross. I got down on my knees and introduced myself. I remember praying to God and asking Him to come into my life so we could get to know each other. Something happened! I actually saw Him and talked to Him for the first time, but this was no ordinary encounter.

What I saw was a majestic and radiant glory that compares to nothing in this world; nothing I had ever seen before or could imagine seeing. I picture a person on top of Mount Everest who can't even open their mouths to utter a word because of the beauty of what is shown before them. What I saw does not begin to compare. It was something so majestic and glorious and beautiful that I can't fathom a description that can identify what was revealed to me in that moment. I saw God! I saw His unending and unconditional love for a son who refused to look at Him for so long. I will try and try throughout this book, but I will never be able to explain what I saw or describe the encounter I had with God that day. What I saw changed my life forever. I saw God, and I saw God because He wanted me to see Him.

There is a big difference in the statements, "I know someone," and, "I have met someone." They are different from each other, but you must have one before you can have the other. With Kim and Cameron, I was able to say that I met them before I was able to say that I knew them. There was no way I could have known God without actually meeting God. When you do meet that person, they become more tangible. They become real.

Maybe you have never seen God the way I saw Him in that crowded arena. Maybe you are just like I was and simply know *who* the author is and have merely been told about His character. Maybe you have confessed Jesus is Lord, and you know the story. You might even say you are a believer. Chances are, you are feeling empty, though. There is nothing that seems real about God. He is distant, and it is impossible for you to see Him. If you can relate to the feelings I have just described, hear this truth. God wants to know you! The creator of the universe WANTS to be tangible for you; He wants to show Himself to you and have a relationship with you.

> *²¹ "Not everyone who says to me, 'Lord, Lord,' will enter the kingdom of heaven, but only the one who does the will of my Father who is in heaven. ²² Many will say to me on that day, 'Lord, Lord, did we not prophesy in your name and in your name drive out demons and in your name perform many miracles?' ²³ Then I will tell them plainly, 'I never knew you. Away from me, you evildoers!'*
>
> Matthew 7:21-23 (New International Version)

I know this passage seems a little harsh, but there is something powerful in it. His statement, "I never knew you," in verse 23 identifies the fact that He *wants* to know you. It's not about the rules you follow, how many Sundays a year you attend church, or how many demons you drive out. It is simply about a relationship. It is about truly knowing the God who made you and being able to see Him, hear Him, and talk to Him. When we experience God in this way, this real and tangible way, it is impossible for us to remain the same. We are changed for eternity.

CHANGED

The unfortunate truth is that some of us never experience this change because we think we know God. We play the part and participate in the routine, but it's all for show. We say we know God, but we can't remember the last time we actually had a real encounter with Him. The worst part, though, is that we don't even notice how blurry our vision of God actually is.

Have you ever gone swimming in a pool and opened your eyes under water? I did this all the time as a kid, and I thought I had these super powers. I could actually swim under water and see where I was going; I was basically a walking, breathing Aqua Man. I know you are not too impressed, but stay with me. I could swim around and see for a while, but after a brief period of time, my eyes would start to burn. I could see without any assistance and felt distinguished and independent. I would glance over at those other kids in the opposite side of the pool with their goggles on, and

I remember feeling so much more superior. Quite frankly, I thought they looked ridiculous.

After a few summers of superior swimming, however, I gave in. My mother brought some goggles in the pool bag, so I gave it a shot thinking it would be a waste of time. I slipped them over my head, put them in position over my eyes, made sure no one was looking, of course, and dove underneath the surface. These… goggles… rocked… my… world! Everything was so clear! I could see distinct lines, shapes, and colors; I could see the barriers of the pool that I could not see before, and dirty spots and stains that were hiding at the bottom were now being revealed. It was incredible how much more I could see, and at the same time, my eyes were not getting burned. I had no idea what I was missing.

Those of us whose hearts are kept hard are the children who refuse to ever accept assistance. We have the mentality that we are powerful and independent, when in reality, we are getting burned out and looking for answers. Most of us probably won't admit how much, but we really do want to see God. We just do not want to ask for help.

What's waiting for us, though, is something incredible. When you do finally see God, something powerful happens. You are new; you are changed.

A lot of people with hardened hearts are deceived into thinking they do not need assistance and that they do not need a savior. The fact is, however, it is not until they are changed that they see how much they actually needed to be saved. Their eyes become open. We see this in the analogy I referred to earlier. The goggles actually helped prove how little I could see before I put them on. I thought I was so powerful! It was not until God revealed Himself, wrecked my pride, softened my heart, and gave me goggles that I could realize how blind I truly was. If it is hard for you to see God, don't be afraid to ask for a little assistance.

BECOMING A REALITY

Here is the good news. Do you remember the characters, the events, the warriors, and everything else I mentioned earlier? Well, all of it is true. I wanted to be just like the people I had heard about in those adventurous stories, and the awesome reality is that I *can* become like one of those characters because the stories are true. It is not just based on a true story as seen in the movies. It actually *is* true, all of it. There is a real God who created real people and constructed real events to take place in order to draw us closer to Him and to bring Himself glory. This is a big God and a real God that you can see and experience. You do not have to be blind anymore and wonder if God really knows you exist. He knows you exist because He created you. Every breath we take is proof that He created us and still has a purpose for us.

There is so much He wants to show us. In Matthew 7:7, He says that all we have to do is ask. Ask, and it will be given to you. This is taken to another level in Jeremiah 29:12-14 where He says, "Then you will call upon me and come and pray to me, and I will listen to you. You will seek me and find me when you seek me with all your heart. I will be found by you and will bring you back from captivity."

If you have never seen God in a real and tangible way, ask Him to reveal Himself to you. Your eyes will be opened, and you will be able to see. You will be able to see Him in everything you do. Spend some time in prayer and ask Him to show you who He is. Seek Him, and He will show Himself to you. The best way to truly see God is to have a real relationship with Him, and it all starts with an introduction.

Chapter 2

Good Teacher

It may take a learning experience to see God.

Every teacher lives, but not every teacher lives forever. This is what separates good teachers from average teachers. Good teachers have the ability to bring out the best in you. They are the teachers that help turn potential into reality. They are the ones that not only provide knowledge but also create an unforgettable learning experience. Good teachers do not believe in failure. They use shortcomings to propel us forward towards success. These are the teachers who push you beyond your limits but are there to catch you when you fall. They prepare you for the next step even when you don't know there *is* one. These teachers believe in you. They may be long gone, but their voice and guidance still ring just when we need it.

When you think about the teachers in your past, there are one or two who probably come to mind. Teachers can take many forms. It may be one of your parents or hopefully both. It may have been your third grade teacher or your football coach. Maybe they were your boss or your best friend. Whatever the case, they are present every time we hear and apply their guidance. They may be physically there or nowhere near us, but their teachings live in us. They move us forward and motivate us to keep going. The teachers you still hear are the ones that will live forever. They are the teachers that are as real and tangible as the first day you met them.

AS A STUDENT

I started school the same way every child starts school, pre-school. I remember going to a pre-school just outside the neighborhood I grew up in, and I remember the day I walked into the building just like it was yesterday. I walked in and was fairly intimidated at first until I caught sight of my best friend who happened to live across the street from me. All the discomfort was gone, and I was ready to go. The fruit loops for breakfast also helped with the comfort issue. There was nothing incredibly special about this school, and we covered everything any pre-school would cover. We learned how to color and tried our hardest to stay within those dreaded borders. We found out how to make friends, who to be friends with, and how to get attention. We had to start with the basics because everything was so new for us as children.

I later went on to primary and elementary school, which was the next big step for me. I then learned how to read by putting words together and took my knowledge further with multiplication tables. Being a talkative little youngster, I also learned the principal's office was not necessarily a privilege, so I learned how to follow authority even when the person was not my mom or dad. I learned in elementary school how to get a girl by playing hide-and-seek with her and calling her your girlfriend; it didn't even matter how many you had! Everything was great, and school was easy for me. Then, I noticed that middle school was right around the corner. I was so scared to take that next step into middle school. I was worried there was going to be no more coloring, and we were just going to write essays all day. I knew the 8th graders were a lot bigger than the 6th graders, and I worried about offending the wrong giant. I was going to have to take geography, algebra, and literature. Was there going to be a recess to play football? Could I still get an ice cream at lunch? I had no idea what to expect.

Middle school came, and it turned out that 6th grade was not too much harder than 5th grade. The building was different along with the hallways, classrooms, teachers, and people, but I could handle it. Plus, I knew that the students I went to school with were in the exact same situation. The only thing that came to be increasingly harder was trying to impress the lady folk. Hide and seek was not quite the same toll it used to be in finding girls. I came to the conclusion that middle school really was not as intimidating as I thought it would be. I actually enjoyed it more. I learned how to talk to girls, how to impress six different teachers instead of one, and what it meant to play ball for a school rather than a recreational team. I learned that there were people in the world who were not too fond of our country while watching the 9/11 attacks in pre-algebra. I also received the knowledge in middle school that there was something called popularity, and if you did not have it, you needed to do whatever it took to get it.

I finally reached the 8th grade, and everything was going my way. I had built up a pretty good reputation by dating some of the prettiest girls, playing on the football team, and I was also one of the smartest people in my class. I felt like a king, but at the same time, I began to look into the near future. I knew high school was just around the corner, and the shadow of fear began to lurk over me once again. I knew I could handle middle school, but high school was going to be a different story. Once again, however, I knew I was going in with everyone else, so I was ready.

I finally reached high school, and I felt so small the first day of school. Academically, I had no idea what was about to happen. I kept going day after day, and it became clear that I was going to be able to do this. What I was learning as a freshmen was not very harsh but more of just a continuation of what I had been learning all my life. The same situations were present with girls and sports with the only differences being the female personnel and the amount of sprints after practice. I was scared once again, but I was also assured once again. I had to take geometry, biology, physics, pre-calculus, and world history, but just like before, I was good at it. The assignments were easy for me, and I knew what it took to make the grades. It was a new school but the same story.

Eventually it came time to begin my college search. As you can probably realize, I became worried about the next step again. This was going to be my biggest step yet and the biggest change yet. I was terrified because a lot of my friends were actually not going to be going through the same transition as me, so I found it hard to relate to someone. I was excited for college but full of fear at the same time. I was going to have to just listen to professors lecture, and I was going to have to actually read a textbook for the first time. Sure, I was a smart kid, but college was going to be very different. Not only was I able to handle college, I absolutely loved it! I had the time of my life getting to know other students, living on my own, dominating in intramurals, and being able to take whatever classes I wanted to take. After changing my mind three or four times, I finally settled on a profession and was able to take only the classes that applied to me. I attended a small church in my college community where I learned how to serve. I learned how to be in a spiritual small group and how to make disciples. I also found God's will for my life and began to pursue that. Along with the academic growth came so much spiritual growth, and it was amazing! It was not as intimidating as I had expected.

A PROCESS

I know that was a long and very repetitive introduction, but it was necessary. There is a purpose for how the schooling process works. There is a reason it seems terrifying to think about college when you are in fourth grade. There are steps that need to be followed, and that is how God created it. What is so interesting about each new step I took in moving up to a higher level of education is that it was never as bad or as intimidating as I had originally expected. I was saying, "God, are you sure?" and He was saying, "Trust me." The reason each level of school was not the monster I expected was because, without even noticing, I was being prepared for the next level of education. The significance of taking pre-algebra in middle school is preparation for taking algebra in high school. The significance of taking algebra as a freshman is preparation for taking advanced algebra and trigonometry as a junior, which is preparation for taking calculus as a senior or in college. You get the point. A lot of times, we do not understand the importance of the process until we get out of the process. Then we look back and say, "Well that makes sense."

It is always intimidating for us to look ahead at the finish line when we are standing at the starting line. We have a lack of confidence because we notice how we could not be further from where we want to be.

One of my favorite shows to watch on television is NBC's *The Biggest Loser*. I love this show because the contestants always seem to achieve what they believe to be impossible. At the beginning of each season, they are so unhealthy and so obese that their lives will be in jeopardy if nothing changes. They come to the ranch and they are excited yet terrified. They want to lose all the weight, but it is almost impossible for them to see themselves in a one hundred and fifty pound body. This is terrifying because they are looking at the final result and have no idea how they are going to get there. This brings another important part of the show into the picture, the two trainers. Every day the trainers lead the contestants in various extreme workouts that push the contestants to their limit.

Before they know it, they are all standing at the season finale in a body that they are proud to show off. They accomplished their goal of gaining their lives back. What is important to see here is that this show does not last a few short weeks. One season takes about 5 or 6 months. These months are months of training, eating right, prioritizing, learning, and following their trainers. It is a process. The workouts get tougher and the contestants become healthier the longer they stay on the ranch. If they completed the same exact workout every day for 6 months, they would not accomplish as much. They lose some weight and are able to complete another set and run another mile; they lose even more and add more sets and run more miles. On the first episode of the last season I watched, the contestants showed up in a desert and were told that they were going to compete in a marathon at the end of the season. Again, they were thinking, "Not a chance." That same episode they were required to run a mile to determine which trainer they would be working with. They almost passed out trying to finish a mile, and they were going to be able to finish a marathon of 26.2 miles after six months? Yes! It was a process and something they had to prepare for. Babies learn to sit up, then they learn to crawl, then they learn to stand on their own, then they learn to walk, then you never stop chasing them. This is how we grow.

We are able to accomplish what we believe to be impossible because, without noticing, we are slowly being prepared for something else, something greater. It is evident in school, it is evident in losing weight, it is evident in learning to walk, and it is evident in our spiritual lives.

SOMEHOW IT HAPPENS

This is a huge reality check because for those of us who think we are unusable by God, He is surely going to use who He wants to use to accomplish His will. He will use you to do something incredible to bring Him glory, but He will not make you do it yourself or hang you out to dry. He promises to walk us through the process and prepare us for what He has called us to do. I had the opportunity to teach Bible classes to public school students. This is something I never thought I would be able to do when I was in high school. I was still relying on making it to the NFL at that point. *Somehow*, I ended up at Berry College, a college without a football program, and had a desire to be a physical education teacher. I started serving at a church and *somehow* ended up as the student director, which required me to read the Bible a lot more and prepare lessons based on scripture. My senior year in college, I was student teaching in a public high school and teaching the gospel on Wednesday nights at church to high school students. *Somehow*, there were absolutely no job opportunities in physical education, and *somehow*, a position opened up to teach the gospel to public school students during regular school days.

I used the word *somehow* repeatedly to show my ignorance in thinking that this was all by chance and mere coincidence. This was no accident. God knew what He wanted to use me for, and He was preparing me for something He was going to accomplish through me. It is was not until after I had this teaching position where I could look back and say, "Oh…. That makes sense!"

Today, I am on staff at a church that is looking to plant another campus in an unreached city. Can you guess who will be leading this new church? I never thought I would be capable of leading a church, but when I look back at everything God used to prepare me for this next step, it all comes together. Every new learning experience has the power to bring us one step closer to Him.

AS A TEACHER

As I referred to earlier, I was blessed with the opportunity to teach Bible classes to public school students. My title was a teacher. When people asked what I did for a living, I told them I was a teacher. When my students looked at me, they saw me as their teacher. When I looked at my paycheck, I was quickly reminded that I got paid like a teacher. Although I was employed as a teacher, I never felt more like a student in my life. I have learned more through teaching than I ever did on the other side of the classroom. I am one of God's students, and He has taught me so much about Himself through this position He assigned to me. There is something crazy about my previous job that makes me feel so much closer to my Father. I had to be in the Word so I knew what I was talking about when giving instruction to my students, but I felt closer to Him in a different way. I feel like I can relate with Him much better, and I'm not trying to compare myself with God. I am just saying He showed me things about Himself through this mission. He is my teacher, and He assigned me to be *their* teacher. I can see God through the way I looked at my students, through the way I helped them teach themselves, and through the way I planned a semester for them to get the most out of it as possible. God revealed Himself to me and showed me the analogy of "a teacher is to students as God is to His children."

MASTER PLANNER

One of the most important jobs a teacher has is planning. At the beginning of each year, the other Christian Learning Center teachers and I got together for a few days for an event called pre-planning. These were the most critical few days of the school year, and no students were present; it was just teachers. The reason for pre-planning is to plan out the entire semester before it even starts. This helped us out and made our jobs easier because, when everything is planned out, there are not as many surprises or "what do I do?" moments. We had a rough outline of what to expect each week of the semester. What was so unique about this planning, though, is that we started with the end; the finish line. We started planning by asking ourselves, "Where do we want our students to be at the end of the semester? What kind of people do we want them to become?"

These things are known as objectives, and they show what the students will be able to do after receiving the instruction. The teachers determine a goal, look at where we want our students to be, and then begin working together to determine the best way to get to that finish line and achieve that goal. It takes a while to plan out four months worth of instruction, but it was worth it because of our hearts for our students. Planning ahead is the best way for teachers and students to achieve goals that are set.

Throughout the semester, I, the teacher, had the vision of where each week and each assignment was going to take us and how one topic was going to lead us into the next. It was my job to keep that vision and to know where we were going to be at the end of the semester. My students, on the other hand, were clueless. They had no idea why they had to complete particular assignments, but it was not their job to know. They did not have the vision. That was my job. Their job was to complete the assignments I gave them and to obey and trust that their teacher knew best. Rarely will teenagers truly think that someone else knows best, but that is their job nonetheless.

I wanted my students to trust me because they should trust me. I gave them every reason to trust me as their teacher. I knew they could accomplish something even when they thought they couldn't. I saw something in them that they couldn't see. What my students did not seem to get was that I would never make them complete an assignment that I thought was impossible for them to complete. They seemed to get the idea that what they were learning was pointless, and it was hard for them to see how they could apply what they had learned to future circumstances. They had no idea, but that was all right because I knew there was a reason for everything they learned.

Teachers sometimes have students take a pre-test for scaling reasons and to determine where the students are when it comes to the material, but this test never usually counts against them. Could you imagine if it did? I would never make my students come in the first day of school and hold them responsible for acing their final exam. There is no logic in that because they have not learned anything yet. It would be impossible for them to be completely competent on a test covering material they have not gone over yet. I know that they *will* know the information and they *will* be equipped with the knowledge and experiences they need to succeed by the time they need to apply it. For this to happen, however, there has to be a process.

ONE STEP IN FRONT OF THE OTHER

We must start with the basics and complete one assignment at a time. We must cover one topic at a time and take one test at a time. When they finish being tested on one topic, we move on to the next topic while still applying the topic we learned before. Again, this is where growth happens; taking one step at a time until we eventually get to where we need to be. The semester has already been planned out since the beginning. The students can't skip steps, they can't jump ahead, and they must keep what they have already acquired. If they were to skip a step or jump ahead in the process, they would miss a crucial ingredient for the recipe and would not be fully equipped to handle what is coming up. Like we observed before, it is my job as the teacher to have the vision and to know the process. It is my students' job to trust and obey, and they will eventually reach where they need to be.

THE PLAN REVEALED

If you have not figured it out yet, there is an incredible parallel here. How many times have we been given a particular assignment or been put in a certain situation and complained about the reasoning? As humans, our favorite word to say to our Father is "Why?" We are all students who freak out because we cannot see where this is going to take us or why we have to do certain things. We want to have it all figured out and see where God is taking us. We want to have the vision, but it is not our job to have the vision. God has already planned out our semester and has already set up the process for us to succeed.

Let's look at the third chapter of the entire Bible in the book of Genesis. Adam and Eve are involved in something known as the fall of man; sounds fun, right? They sin against God and have to suffer the consequences. God's mercy is shown through this situation by not destroying them on the spot, but He goes even further and provides something that is indescribable; something we can't fathom. He gives them something they do not deserve, and for the first time in the Bible, He reveals His amazing grace. Let's jump in the 15th verse of chapter 3 in the book of Genesis where

Adam and Eve have already confessed their sin to God. God is addressing the serpent and telling him what the plan is:

"And I will put enmity
  between you and the woman,
  and between your offspring and hers;
he will crush your head,
  and you will strike his heel."

Genesis 3:15 (NIV)

This is an overlooked verse in scripture, but this is the first time God tells us His plan. He gives us a promise. The last sentence is huge; *"he will crush your head and you will strike his heel."* When God uses the pronoun, "he", He is referring to Jesus. This is at the very beginning of all creation with the only two humans on the planet, and God is already mentioning Jesus. The serpent will strike Jesus' heel, but Jesus is going to crush the serpent's head by defeating him on the cross to bring salvation for His children. Adam and Eve, along with the rest of God's chosen people, will still be able to be reconciled and reunited with Him forever. God has already planned it out! The story has already been written, and the process has already been constructed. He had the vision ever since light came flashing out of His mouth. He is the creator, and it is His job to have the vision.

We have one of two problems as students. Some of us have the problem of lacking confidence. This is a problem because it leads us to stagnancy. We feel as though we are incapable of completing certain assignments, so we do not even attempt them out of fear. This shows how little trust we have in our teacher. He knows we can even when we think we can't. The other problem some of us have is having too much confidence. This is a problem because it leads us to skipping steps and jumping ahead of our teacher. As mentioned earlier, this leads us to missing crucial ingredients and not being equipped with what we need to accomplish God's will. Both extremes reflect our desire to control God's plan. We get caught up in trying to be the teacher when God wants us to be the student. We are constantly trying to make God follow our lesson plan when He knows the only way we can succeed and arrive where we need to be is to follow His. We want reasons for completing assignments when God does not need us to know the reasons. It is not our job, as students, to have the vision. Our job is simple; trust and obey.

Education is not required to see God, but it is completely possible for God to be revealed through it. A law may say that we have to keep God out of our schools, but in order for us to keep God out of something, we have to be able to contain Him in something. The problem (or not a problem at all in this case) is that our God can't be contained by anything. God is going to reveal Himself wherever He pleases. God can be seen in every learning experience; it is just about focusing our eyes to see Him. The way we experience growth through a step-by-step and planned out process is the same way we experience growth in our relationship with Him. The way teachers see their students, in many ways, is the same way God looks at His students. The same way school semesters are planned out by having the end in mind first is the same way God planned out the process of us eventually being reunited with Him in the end for all of eternity. Everything in our educational system reflects the character and glory of God and reveals His plan for His students. All we have to do for Him to reveal Himself in this real and tangible way is have faith and do our job. Our job is simple; trust and obey our Good Teacher.

Chapter 3

Competitive-Natured
It may take a battle to see God.

Everything we are exposed to in this world pushes us to compete with one another. We compete for jobs, we compete for money, we compete for approval, and too often, we compete for love. Let me be clear by saying that this kind of competing will never lead us to God. Competing pushes us into comparing, and comparing leads us down two possible roads. One of these roads is the highway of pride. The other road is worthlessness. Pride leads to our neglect of the need of God's Holy Spirit. Worthlessness, which is different than humility, leads to a belief that Christ's blood does not contain enough power to save us. Neither of these roads lead to Jesus.

When we begin comparing ourselves to everyone else, we start associating our self-worth with our performance. If you don't succeed, win the girl, or get the promotion, you are not as valuable as the person who did. If you did come out on top, you have more worth than the person you defeated. Do you see the problem here? This mindset will cause us to become either depressed or obsessed. This is not why God created us, and this is not what Jesus went to the cross for.

The only thing that accurately determines our value is the cross. God revealed how valuable we were to Him the moment He sent His only Son to take our place on the cross. This is not something we can compete for. It was freely given to us. Paul tells us in Ephesians 2 that it is by grace, through faith we have been saved and not by works. God fought for you and me a long time ago so we wouldn't *have* to compete with each other. There is nothing we can do to make Him love us any more or any less than He already does. His love is unconditional and permanent.

Although we should stay away from competing with each other, God can definitely use our spirit of competition for His glory. There is a difference between competing *with* each other and competing *for* each other. When God sent Jesus to conquer Satan and death, He was competing *for* us. When you are competing for something, you are fighting for something. God fought for us by laying down His own life for us. Truly seeing Him may come through fighting for Him the same way He fought for us.

THERE IS NO "I" IN TEAM

Looking back on my childhood, it is extremely hard to remember a time period where I was not involved in some sort of recreational activity. Autumn brought my love for football. Soon after fall came winter, where I signed up for basketball. Hoops season was quickly followed by spring and the season of baseball. Summer was about the only time I had a break, but I would also frequently participate in summer soccer leagues. Talk about a sports nut, right? As I got older, I dropped a couple sports and really focused on baseball and football which were the more dominant sports being in the South. When I reached high school, football had captured my heart and won my undivided attention.

It was not until I reached college and started pursuing coaching that I came to a new and more permanent view on sports. Growing up, you always hear about the aspect of a team and how it is about the team and not the individual. Together Everyone Achieves More! You get the picture. It is fairly easy to understand that a team or a group of people is a lot harder to defeat than a single individual. This is common sense that athletes are taught at a very young age. What I have found to be remarkable, however, is how much the aspect of a team relates to God and His purpose in creating so many unique individuals.

I will be using the illustration of a football team to communicate this idea because of my own experiences with the sport, but the application applies to any sport or activity that requires a team to succeed. In high school, I remember our coaches used to always express how football was the ultimate team sport. There are many aspects to a football team, but we are solely going to concentrate on the offensive part of a team. A typical offense consists of about four linemen and a center. These are usually the largest and meanest men on the field, and they are great for getting any obstacle out of the way. There is also a tight end that is, basically, a lineman with slightly more skillful agility. These are big guys who can run and catch along with their blocking abilities. Then you have a running back, known as the tail back, and a full back. The full back is a man built like a fridge and is good for busting through the brick wall of a defense and creating a whole for the tail back. The tail back's job is to get the ball to the end zone as quickly as possible without being stopped by the defense. An offense will also have a couple of wide receivers. These players are not incredible blockers but are great for speed and provide the option to get more yards by way of passing the ball. Finally, you have the team's conductor, the quarterback. The quarterback is the leader of the offense and is the brains behind each play. Every good offense needs a good quarterback. This completes a typical offense for any football team. It is complete with eleven guys who vary in size, athletic ability, speed, and assignments. The characteristics may sound random, but it is a perfect combination of abilities to be successful.

Now that we have the basic outline of a football team's offense, let me explain the biased opinions of my former coaches about football being the ultimate team sport. As we have just seen, there are many different positions on a football team, and these positions are assigned based on the abilities of the athlete. Some athletes are big, some are small, some are fast, others are strong, some are smarter or more experienced and have more responsibility while others are great at accomplishing one thing. This is easily seen at any sporting event you may attend. There will always be different sizes, shapes, and abilities for each athlete participating. Have you ever really thought about it? Have you ever thought about how all these various aspects seem to work together so efficiently? Going back to football, there is a reason each player is at his particular position. You would never see a 300-pound man running down the field trying to catch a pass from the quarterback. It is actually quite hilarious to see because it does not fit! A 300-pound man belongs on a line to be used as an obstacle.

Although an offense is comprised of many different kinds of athletes with various gifts and abilities, for one play to be successful, all of these diverse gifts and abilities must come together at the same time to achieve the desired goal. On a given play, the receiver has his job, the tight end has another job, the guards and tackles have their jobs, and so on. A successful play comes from a successful team that is able to use their different abilities to come together as one unit. I remember daydreaming when I was younger and thinking one of these chain thoughts in my head, "The center is the most important player because without him snapping the ball, nothing will happen... I suppose the quarterback is more important though because he has to take the ball and do something with it… I guess he can't really do anything with it if no one blocks for him… If he does give the ball to someone else, the running back has to take the hand off, or the receiver has to catch the ball…"

It just kept going on and on because I was beginning to realize how each player has a part in helping the team succeed. I finally noticed that it was not really up to one specific player, but every player was equal in significance. Some were just noticed more than others. If one piece of the puzzle was off or did not complete his job based on the abilities he had, the team would not succeed or achieve their goal. Another term that can be used to describe this idea is *irreducible complexity.* Irreducible complexity is a scientific term that says there are some organisms that, when divided into different parts and having some of the parts taken out, cannot function. The team is the organism, the different parts are the players, and when those parts are taken out, the team cannot function properly.

Let's look at what God says about this in His word. In 1 Corinthians 12, Paul writes to the people at Corinth and is explaining to them how we are all gifted in different ways. We were built with extremely unique abilities, but that truth does not diminish our significance. He goes on and elaborates a bit further:

> *Just as a body, though one, has many parts, but all its many parts form one body, so it is with Christ. [13] For we were all baptized by one Spirit so as to form one body— whether Jews or Gentiles, slave or free— and we were all given the one Spirit to drink. [14] Even so the body is not made up of one part but of many.*
>
> *[15] Now if the foot should say, "Because I am not a hand, I do not belong to the body," it would not for that reason stop being part of the body. [16] And if the ear should say, "Because I am not an eye, I do not belong to the body," it would not for that reason stop being part of the body. [17] If the whole body were an eye, where would the sense of hearing be? If the whole body were an ear, where would the sense of smell be? [18] But in fact God has placed the parts in the body, every one of them, just as he wanted them to be. [19] If they were all one part, where would*

the body be? [20] As it is, there are many parts, but one body.

[21] The eye cannot say to the hand, "I don't need you!" And the head cannot say to the feet, "I don't need you!" [22] On the contrary, those parts of the body that seem to be weaker are indispensable,[23] and the parts that we think are less honorable we treat with special honor. And the parts that are unpresentable are treated with special modesty, [24] while our presentable parts need no special treatment. But God has put the body together, giving greater honor to the parts that lacked it, [25] so that there should be no division in the body, but that its parts should have equal concern for each other. [26] If one part suffers, every part suffers with it; if one part is honored, every part rejoices with it.

1 Corinthians 12:12-26 (NIV)

The aspect of a team is powerful! Think about your sport: football, baseball, basketball, volleyball, hockey, track and field... Think about your body... your eyes, your hands, your mouth and nose, your brain and nerves... Think about your work place: the CEO, the manager, accounting, sales, human resources... Think about your family: the father, the mother, the son, the daughter... Think about the disciples: the bold, the doubter, the betrayer, the fishermen, and the tax collectors. God had a special design for a team all along. He has created each of us exactly how He wanted us to accomplish the purpose He has for us. God created the body of the church, every single aspect of it. It is not by chance that there is not one pair of identical fingerprints even with identical twins. Psalm 139 reveals this truth:

> *For you created my inmost being;*
> *you knit me together in my mother's womb.*
> *I praise you because I am fearfully and wonderfully made;*
> *your works are wonderful, I know that full well.*
>
> Psalm 139:13-14 (NIV)

He set up His team the way He wanted it and assigned each athlete their position based on the gifts and abilities He gave them. He is the coach. He is supreme. It is His team, and that is why the glory will always belong to HIM.

STEPPING INTO BATTLE

Every coach is guilty of using this line at least once in their career, "Men (or women), when you step out on that field (or court), you are stepping into battle!" What a motivational tactic! That sentence has a magical power of bringing your adrenaline to a whole new level. You know you will be competing, and in most cases, you know it will not be your last chance to compete. The people who have a good head on their shoulders and who are in touch with reality always say, "It's only a game." This is a truth that anyone NOT in the competition will quickly and easily agree with, but it could not be any further from the truth for those who are about to step into the competition. Speaking as a former athlete, it *is* just a game, but it is *not* just a game. Stay with me. The actual game does not matter too much; the outcome of the game will not define who you are for eternity. One style of competition is really not even more important than any other style of competition. It is only a game… but it is not.

As soon as the coach utters those words, "…you are stepping into battle," everything changes. It is no longer just a game. It is serious, personal, and time for business. Let's think about a military battle for a moment. To those soldiers, it is not *just* a battle. It is a mission and an opportunity. They have an opportunity to complete the mission and bring glory to their country. I am not trying to praise or glorify battle by any means. My goal is simply to point out one of the most interesting things about a battle. The side that wins is usually the side who has more motivation. Where does the motivation come from? The motivation is deeply routed in the heart of every soldier. Contrary to belief, it has nothing to do with the other side, the other nation, or the other team. The motivation comes from who we are representing and what we are fighting for. Soldiers in the military are not in battle fighting for themselves; they are serving and representing their country. This truth motivates them to keep fighting and to keep going further than they thought they could go.

Now, bringing it back to the pre-game locker room chat, that is why the idea of stepping into battle makes an athlete's hands start sweating and limbs start shaking. Their level of motivation has risen to an incredible level, and they don't even know how it happens. This is because it comes natural for us to want to fight for something. For the athlete, they are fighting to represent their team, their school, their family, their community, their region, their state, and their home. It has nothing to do with the individuals on the other side, who their mascot is, or where they're from. It is not about who we are fighting *against*; it all comes from who and what we are fighting *for*. It comes from who we are representing. Our hometown high school baseball team just won the Georgia AAAA state championship. Being a graduate for some years now, I have no idea who any of the players are on the team, but for some reason, deep inside of me, there is this pride for the city of Loganville and where I came from. I had absolutely nothing to do with the team winning the crown, but I am still proud to say *our* team won. *We* won. Whether the athletes knew it or not they were playing and fighting for something much bigger than themselves. Their motivation did not come from who they were playing against but who they were playing for. It is not just a game. It is a battle for glory, and it comes natural for us to want to compete in it.

This is such a beautiful picture of how God wired us. Whether we know it or not, like a soldier and an athlete, we are in the middle of a battle. It is not something we signed up for or voluntarily enlisted into. It is something we were born into. As soon as each one of us came out of the womb and took our first breath, we stepped into battle. This was not by choice but by intelligent design.

IN THE BEGINNING

Let me paint a scene for us. Picture yourself in the middle of Wal-Mart. There is a mother with her child walking through the store with a shopping cart. You are an innocent by-stander just listening. Suddenly, you hear the child express their desire for a certain item whether it is a toy, candy bar, or something flashy that has caught their attention. They begin to beg and plead for this new item that they absolutely cannot live without. The parent knows the child does not need the item, so the mother tells the child, "No." The child then begins to scream crying out to the mother and throwing a huge fit. The child is arguing, the mother is arguing, and a battle is created. We are all aware of this scene whether we have seen it or heard it. There is a battle because the child wants something that the parent does not want the child to have, and the child's natural response is to rebel.

The same thing would happen all the time in my classroom at school. I would tell a student to change seats for a specific reason, and their immediate reaction was to ask why. I wanted them to do something that they did not want to do, so a battle was created. The students thought I was just trying to make their life more difficult and take away all their fun. In reality, I knew that my decision would actually benefit them more. They would get more out of the class, stay out of trouble, and would probably find the class to be more enjoyable. They may not have understood why I wanted something done, but it was not their job to understand my reasoning. It is so common because it comes natural for us to want to rebel against our authority. If you are still not convinced, we can take this truth all the way back to the beginning of time.

We refer to Satan as the ultimate enemy, but this was not always the case. God created Satan to be something amazing and beautiful. The problem was that Satan did not want to sit under God's authority; he wanted more. Because of his rebellion, Satan lost it all. Finally, we come to when God created the first human beings, Adam and Eve. He made them different than anything else and gave them everything they could ever want. He game them the plants, the animals, the land, and most importantly, a mind. He gifted them with the ability to make decisions and choices. He supplied them with everything, but the only thing that God wanted Adam and Eve to stay away from was this ONE tree. You can have everything, but this one little thing is off limits. How did the enemy respond? He asked, "Why not *that* apple on *that* one tree? Why can't you have *that*?" The two humans had everything on the planet, but they were tricked into desiring the one thing God said no to. Where did this come from? Satan was the first to go against authority, so he is the master of rebellion. He comes in to this scene in the form of a serpent and begins stirring things up. He did not focus on all the good things they had been given. He wanted them to focus on the one thing their authority said no to. "Who is God to say you can't do that? He is being mean, not letting you act on your own, and not treating you like an adult. He is holding you back from what you can do and be."

Sound familiar? A battle is created.

God says *this*; Satan says *that*. God gives a command and Satan asks why. Adam and Eve, meanwhile, are in the middle of this battle between good and evil, life and death, the flesh and the Spirit. Why did God tell them not to eat the apple? He told them not to because bad stuff would happen if they did! He did not want to make life more difficult or try to take away all their fun. He wanted the absolute best for His children, and He knew something they didn't. Their job was not to understand God's reasoning, but their job was to trust and obey. God said no; Satan said yes. There are two sides waging war against each other and a battle is created.

Paul understood the idea of a battle probably more than anyone else in history. He spent most of his time in prisons suffering for the name of Christ. He sent letters to many churches and individuals while in prison, and there is one particular letter I want to look at. Paul wrote a letter to the Romans, and in chapter six, he explains this battle.

> *Don't you know that when you offer yourselves to someone as obedient slaves, you are slaves of the one you obey — whether you are slaves to sin, which leads to*

death, or to obedience, which leads to righteousness?

Romans 6:16 (ESV)

Again, there are two sides: death and righteousness. He goes further in the letter to chapter seven where he shows us how he is feeling in this battle:

[14] We know that the law is spiritual; but I am unspiritual, sold as a slave to sin. [15] I do not understand what I do. For what I want to do I do not do, but what I hate I do. [16] And if I do what I do not want to do, I agree that the law is good. [17] As it is, it is no longer I myself who do it, but it is sin living in me. [18] For I know that good itself does not dwell in me, that is, in my sinful nature.[c] For I have the desire to do what is good, but I cannot carry it out. [19] For I do not do the good I want to do, but the evil I do not want to do—this I keep on doing. [20] Now if I do what I do not want to do, it is no longer I who do it, but it is sin living in me that does it. [21] So I find this law at work: Although I want to do good, evil is

> *right there with me. ²² For in my inner being I delight in God's law;²³ but I see another law at work in me, waging war against the law of my mind and making me a prisoner of the law of sin at work within me.*

Romans 7:14-23 (ESV)

You may want to read that again to get all the "want to do's and not want to do's" in order. It is kind of confusing, but we see a major battle here. Paul is basically saying, "I want to serve and be obedient to God, but I have this rebellious heart that wants to go against that." He even explains how two sides are waging war against each other. As humans, we are born into sin. It is in our blood. Then, God reveals Himself to us and shows us something so incomparably better. The only thing is that just because we are now on the winning team or have chosen a certain path does not mean that there is no longer a battle. When or if you became a Christian, you did not just get out of the game. You simply became a member of the other team. The only thing that changed was who you were fighting for.

BRINGING IT ALL TOGETHER

I've said it many times already, and I will continue to repeat myself. God is all about His glory. When we face trials and finally overcome them, God put them in place to bring us back to Him or closer to Him. It was ultimately to glorify Himself. That is why God does everything He does. It is not by accident that we are in a battle. God is not surprised that He was rebelled against. He is all knowing. He has written the story, dotted the period, and closed the book. We are in a battle because God wants us to be and because it will ultimately bring Him glory.

The beauty of the battle is who and what we are fighting for. As humans, we fight for the things we love, and we fight hard. The harder we fight usually determines the amount of love we have for who we are fighting for. God designed us to have this competitive nature because He wants to be fought for. Our God is a jealous God who is all about His glory, and He wants us to fight for Him because what we fight for is what we love. He knows we cannot win the battle. That is why He already took care of that part when He sent His son to the cross. He has already defeated the enemy and crushed the head of the serpent so that we don't have to. The outcome is determined, but He still wants us to compete. The only thing different about this battle should be our level of anxiety. Unlike sports or a war between nations, we are blessed enough to already know the outcome. We have won and can now fight with confidence in the One who sent us. Like I stated earlier in the chapter, He has already equipped us with what we need to compete. We all have certain gifts and are called to play a certain position.

Every time that pre-game moment comes where your palms get sweaty, your fingertips and legs start shaking, and your adrenaline starts pumping, you are getting ready for battle. You are becoming motivated and getting ready to compete for something. God starts to become more and more tangible through the moistness of your hands and through the feeling of your nerves racing. When a soldier goes into battle, he is fighting for something tangible and real. When an athlete steps into competition, he is representing something that is tangible and real. As followers of Christ, we are now ambassadors. An ambassador is someone who is the representative of something else. Paul explains how we are now ambassadors of Christ and His name. In this battle, we are called to compete and to represent our team and our coach who just happens to be the creator of the universe and everything in it. It is amazing how tangible and real God becomes in the spirit of competition. It is not just a game. Who are you fighting for?

Chapter 4

A Little More Conversation
It may take a conversation to see God.

About three and a half years ago, I had one of the best conversations of my life. I was in college and was attending a night of worship our church was holding. Kim was there, and we were still in the "make it or break it" part of the relationship. We had just met a few days prior in our church's coffee shop, so the butterflies and nerves were still peaking in both of us. We had not really spent any one-on-one time with each other yet, so I asked her if she wanted to go get some coffee after the night of worship. Unfortunately, Kim is not much of a coffee drinker, so we settled for grabbing a quick bite to eat at the local waffle house. I got game, right? Our first date…waffle house. In my defense it was pretty late after worship, and there was not much of a selection to choose from at that time of the night in Rome, Georgia. What was even greater was that she had already eaten, so our first date turned into her watching me devour an all-star special which we all know to be an attractive experience. Nonetheless, those little details seemed to evaporate the moment we started speaking.

I'll spare you every topic we journeyed through in this conversation, but we ended up sitting in that waffle house for a good three hours. There wasn't a moment of awkward silence or trying to figure out the perfect combination of words to say. Every word and thought came so naturally and thirty minutes transformed into three hours. We were laughing, connecting, and learning, and I'll never forget it. I mentioned in chapter one what I was thinking before I actually met Kim and how amazing it was the first time we met, but this conversation brought everything to a new level. Our new friendship was more real. I had a better understanding of who she was, what she believed, and where she came from. I left that conversation counting down the hours until I would be able to do it again. It was an indescribable feeling, and if you have ever had such a conversation with someone, you know exactly what I'm talking about. You leave with giddiness because you actually connected with someone, you share similar beliefs, and you can see this relationship going somewhere. It's the kind of conversation that makes you want to be a better person because the experience was genuine.

Kim's existence became more real to me after that night because of our conversation. I could now describe her in a way that I never could before because I knew things about her now. I knew how she felt about certain issues, what some of her pet peeves were, and whether she preferred writing a paper or taking a test. All of those little things about her seem like useless details, but altogether, they make up everything this woman is. It all came out of a series of conversations. It is three and a half years later, and I am still in love with those conversations that we have.

WHERE COMPUTERS FAIL

There is something powerful about a conversation that you can't get anywhere else. I could have easily gone onto Kim's Facebook and found out the same information that she communicated to me. I could have seen who her family was, what high school she went to, what kind of music she liked, and much more, but something would have been missing; the most important thing…her. I could have researched who she was, but that would have spared Kim the joy of telling me herself. When I got Kim's engagement ring, I was informed not to show anyone. This was extremely difficult and seems a bit unnecessary, but I would have taken something away from Kim. I would have taken away the joy of her showing off the ring herself on *her* finger and seeing all of her friends and family react when they saw it. There is something extremely special about being able to show something or share something with someone else.

Without having a physical conversation, we wouldn't have been able to see each other's reactions and expressions. I would have missed out on looking into those beautiful green eyes, smelling the scent of her perfume, or hearing her gentle voice. The conversation provided a way for both of us to connect, and it made getting to know the other person tangible. It gave me the opportunity to tell other people about who Kim was in a way where they had no choice but to believe she was a real person. When I told my best friends about the girl I had an amazing conversation with, none of them said, "Well, I just don't believe in her. I don't think she's a real thing." No. They believed how I felt about this person and could not wait to meet her. I don't think I would have gotten the same reaction if I had told them about a girl I stalked on Facebook.

Many of you know exactly what I am talking about because you are in that relationship where you feel like no other two people have the conversations the two of you share. The power of a conversation is easy to detect in romantic relationships, but they are powerful in other relationships as well. Think of anyone in your life that is important to you and think of why they are important to you. A lot of my best friends are so important to me because of the conversations we have had and the experiences we have shared. I am able to laugh with them, struggle with them, and express myself to them. I love getting together with my old college buddies because we spend most of the time reminiscing on past experiences. We all sit around a fire and the words "Remember when…" are spoken. We'll bring up an old conversation or something hysterical somebody said, and then we'll burst into laughter. I cherish the relationships I have with these guys because we have shared so much with each other. If I was struggling with something, I could have a simple conversation with one of those guys to find he had recently been through a similar experience. It is incredible how a conversation can help two people relate with one another.

There is also something powerful about the tangibility of words being spoken. There is a distinct difference between assuming information and being told information. Think of your family or someone extremely close to you. You may know that they love you, but doesn't it mean so much more when they tell you they love you? Kim should know that I love her because of what I do for her. I am there to lead her, protect her, and serve her, and all of that is necessary in a relationship, but she also needs me to tell her how I enjoy doing it. I need to be able to show her how much I love her, but I also need to tell her how much I love her. The assurance of me communicating my love to her is necessary and helps her to know without any doubt how I feel about her. Think about how special it was the first time you said, "I love you" to that person in your life. There is a reason that communication and conversations like that are so powerful in relationships. It makes the other person's existence more real and tangible. You can feel it.

THE DISCONNECT

Have you ever known someone with a phone voice? These are the people who could be yelling in anger, crying uncontrollably, or in the middle of deep sleep, but as soon as the phone rings, everything changes. They perk up instantly with an emphatic and cheerful, "Hello!" They have the power to change the tone of their voice immediately. Meanwhile, those of us witnessing the climate change are left wondering, "Who the heck is this person?"

I have to confess and say that I do the same thing when it comes to prayer. I find myself at times having a prayer voice, and I don't think I'm the only one. I strategically used the term "conversation" for the title of this chapter because there is a certain expectation when it comes to "prayer." Prayer has turned into memorizing a set number of sentences that we say before meals, sporting events, and going to bed. This is the very thing that makes prayer so intimidating for most of us. With expectations come fears of not meeting those expectations. What if I don't do it right? What if it's too short? What if it's too long? What if I don't sound religious enough?

I can't help but notice how much I use my prayer voice when it comes to talking to God. Often times, it doesn't seem much like a conversation. It seems more like a ritual or a routine. It seems fake. I also can't help but wonder if God is the One left wondering who *this* person is. Where is the guy who was just broken by the loss of his child? Where is the mother who I know is overwhelmed and completely exhausted? God isn't interested in our fake and meaningless small talk. He wants the three-hour Waffle House conversation. He wants the real you.

There is a disconnect when it comes to how we talk to each other and how we talk to God. Can you imagine taking a whole day and speaking to everyone in prayer voice? How weird would that be? What if we turned it around, though? What if we used our real, vulnerable, and conversational voice when talking with God? When Jesus told us that His burden is easy and His yoke is light, He was trying to convince us to come to Him. He wants us to come and dump all of our junk as if we were doing the same with a friend over a cup of coffee. He wants us to share ourselves with Him.

NO MORE SECRETS

It is no accident we find comfort in sharing ourselves with someone else. God built and wired each of us with the desire to seek out relationships. Why would God make us that way? It is because God actually *wants* to be your friend, and He wants to be in a relationship with you. Check out the evidence.

> *"I've told you these things for a purpose: that my joy might be your joy, and your joy wholly mature. This is my command: Love one another the way I loved you. This is the very best way to love. Put your life on the line for your friends. You are my friends when you do the things I command you. I'm no longer calling you servants because servants don't understand what their master is thinking and planning. No, I've named you friends because I've let you in on everything..."*
>
> John 15:11-15 (The Message)

Jesus is speaking here, and He is explaining His love for you and me. He is letting us in on everything. There is nothing He is hiding or keeping from us. He is sharing His deepest desires with us and telling us ahead of time He loves us so much that He is going to jump in front of the bullet for us. You won't find a greater friend than that. Jesus finds joy in being our friend, and He wants us to feel the same way about being *His* friend. Again, He wants us to share with Him the way He did with us. He wants us to let Him in on everything! He wants to know our deepest thoughts and desires, and He wants us to be completely open with Him and not hold anything back. He wants us to, and He tells us to!

> *"Ask and it will be given to you; seek and you will find; knock and the door will be opened to you.*
>
> Matthew 7:7 (NIV)

> *"For I know the plans I have for you," declares the LORD, "plans to prosper you and not to harm you, plans to give you hope and a future. Then you will call on me and come and pray to me, and I will listen to you. You will seek me and find me when you seek me with all your heart."*
>
> Jeremiah 29:11-13 (NIV)

I love this passage because it shows God's intention from the beginning. When He says, "You will find me when you seek me with all your heart," it shows that He is opening the door for us to find Him and to see Him in a way that leaves us completely vulnerable and exposed. God's Word constantly reveals that He wants to be found by you and me. He wants the kind of relationship where you can talk about anything. Think of any time you have had to describe the person you're closest with to someone else. It usually always includes the statement, "I can talk to that person about anything." Whether it is a parent, grandparent, spouse, sibling, or friend, the people we are closest to are the people we can most easily talk to. They are the people who understand us and see us in a way no one else can. God wants us to have those people in our lives; He's the One who blesses us with those people. The most important aspect to understand here, however, is that as much as it thrills God for us to have someone to go to, He wants us to go to Him even more. He wants us to seek *Him* out and find *Him* and talk to *Him*.

A FITTING FATHER

A lot of Christians refer to God as a father. It is one of His many names. Father. If you can, I want you to picture what a father is. I'm not talking about the deadbeats and men who did not have enough courage to step into that role. I'm talking about a father who is there for his family, loves his family and leads his family. I always picture a great father as one who loves spending time with his children. He loves listening to them and talking with them. If it is hard for you to picture a father of your own, I have a back-up plan for you. Try thinking of Danny Tanner from the show *Full House*. What a great show, right? Danny was a man who, unfortunately, lost his wife and now had the task of raising three adorable daughters with the help of his brother and best friend (not the easiest task in the world). Every show had the exact same timeline of events. The specific details varied each episode, but the outline was extremely consistent.

Allow me to explain: The show would start, a situation would be introduced, the three daughters would, in some way, get between a rock and a hard place, there would be a climax of something going wrong, and then came the solution. I know this seems like a huge tangent, but stay with me. I want to focus on the solution part of the show. I started noticing a pattern every time it came to this part. Things would get about as bad as they could get and then Danny, the father, would come to the rescue. He would step into the girls' room, have a seat on their bed, the soft music in the background would start playing, and a conversation would take place. The girls would try to tell him what was going wrong and how they were feeling as they tried to handle the situation on their own. Danny would just sit there patiently listening as they poured everything out. Then it was his turn. He would show his understanding of how they felt and give a wise word of advice as their relationship grew to an unprecedented level. You would leave every episode feeling uplifted and encouraged knowing that everything worked out and life was back to normal in the Tanner house.

Now I understand that the reality of life is quite different from this Hollywood television show, but the picture the show painted of a loving father being their for his children is pretty accurate to the intention of our Father in heaven. A father and his children grow closer together in the presence of powerful conversations. It does not just occur in the show, *Full House*. Think of any show or movie. The most intimate moments between a child and their father are found during the bedside conversations. Great fathers live for these moments with their children when they can simply just be with them, listen to them, and talk with them.

Another characteristic of great fathers is that they know what is best for their children. They want perfection for their children. So if we look at God as our father, He knows what is best for His children. We are nowhere near perfect, and our Father knows that. Now, since God is the only One who *is* perfect, He knows that what's best for us, His children, is HIM. This is why God wants to be your closest friend. He wants you to come to Him bringing all your junk with you and laying it at His feet. He is calling out saying, "I love you. Tell me about it. How does that make you feel? What if we handled it this way? Try looking at it with this point of view. Etc."

God wants to have such an intimate relationship with you. He wants you to seek Him and find Him. He wants you to be fully satisfied when you come to Him. Strong buildings are built by stacking one powerful brick after another. Strong relationships are built by having one powerful conversation after another. Praying to God is not about trying to impress Him by saying a required combination of words. It's about coming to Him fully exposed and having a conversation with Him that makes His presence more tangible. This is hard, and this is why Jesus gave us some help when He told us how to pray in Matthew 6. It is possible to speak truth and be real at the same time. Here is an example of how Jesus' led prayer can lead us into being real with God.

Our Father, Lord in Heaven, hallowed be your name- "God, I am praising your name above my name even though I struggle with selfishness."

Let your kingdom come, your will be done on Earth as it is in Heaven- "Father, this is hard for me because I have a will of my own. Please help me remember that your will is always going to be better than my will."

Give us this day our daily bread- "Lord, I spend way too much time worrying about how much stuff I have and my need for more. Help me to realize that you are my provision and you are enough for me day by day."

Forgive us our debts, as we also have forgiven our debtors- "Jesus, I expect so much forgiveness from you while I'm angry at others. Help me have the same compassion on them that I desire from you. It is hard for me to let certain things go, but I know that, with you, I can do anything."

Lead us not into temptation, but deliver us from evil- "Father, I struggle with temptation every day. In these times, I have failed before. In these times, I need your strength in place of my weakness. Please open up my eyes, and keep me from being deceived again."

Jesus did not give us this gift of a prayer simply to be memorized. He was leading us into the presence of God with a pure heart. The Lord's Prayer is supposed to ignite our prayer lives, not cheapen it.

Kim's presence did not feel tangible or real to me until I sat down in that waffle house and had a life-changing conversation with her. God's presence will continue to feel as distant as it does until you take the time to sit down and have a conversation with Him. Trust me. When you seek Him with all your heart, you will find Him because He is already waiting on you and wants to be found by you. I encourage you to put this book aside for a minute, and take some time to talk and listen to the God who knows you better than anyone. What you experience could open your eyes and be the first step to life change.

Chapter 5

Open The Blinds
It may take stepping outside to see God.

One of the most precious chapters of my life is the time I spent in college. You always here people talk about how their college years were some of the best years of their lives. This pattern was no different for me. As I mentioned earlier, I was fortunate enough to attend Berry College in Rome, GA. I made friends with some of the most incredible people you could meet, kept my stomach full with plenty of Waffle House, got involved with a great church, met the woman of my dreams, and ended up with a fairly prestigious education. These were all incredible experiences, but the most valuable thing I was able to take away from those years was the intimate time I spent with God.

For those of you who did not know this little fact, Berry College is the largest campus in the world when speaking of land area. Berry's land consists of roughly 26,000 acres. What is even more interesting is that while I was enrolled, there was just shy of 2,000 total students enrolled. Do the math. That leaves each student with about 14 acres to call their own. To an average college student, that may sound like the most boring place on Earth. For me, however, that campus became my sanctuary, my escape, and my home. It was the perfect place to get away.

HOUSE OF DREAMS

Out of the thousands of acres the college campus provided, a portion of it quickly captured my heart. Martha Berry, the founder of the school, had a house that her students had built on the top of a mountain on campus. It is now called the House of Dreams. Every now and then, when school and the stress of life got the best of me, I would make the ten-minute drive back to mountain campus, hike up the forty-five-minute trail to the house, and fall into a hammock that I believe God Himself placed in the perfect spot. If I could, I would get you to close your eyes as I described this setting for you, but seeing that you need your eyes to read makes that request pointless. Maybe we can try that in a bit, but I'll describe this place as best as I can.

The house sat at the very top of a mountain, which seemed to be looking over all the rest of the aspiring hills and gave me the ability see for miles. As I would lie in the hammock that was gently swaying back and forth, my arm would hang over the side with my hand lightly petting the blades of grass as if my fingers couldn't get enough of nature's smooth carpet. There would be a light breeze in the eighty-degree air that had just enough presence to keep me from sweating. These elements were intoxicating and contributed to the experience, but what kept me coming back was the painting I was able to embrace. It was as if Thomas Kinkaid set up shop right in front of me, only better. It was in the heart of October, and the miles of trees were just beginning to turn. There was an ocean of yellows, greens, light oranges and reds that rolled over the hills. The sun had already begun its descent as the sky took on a clear, pale blue. A giant oak tree stood strong just to the side with a branch creeping over the sky creating the perfect frame for this picture. It was as if God had just finished a masterpiece, set down His palette, and said, "Enjoy!"

YOUR PERFECT SETTING

We have all been outside some time or another. All of us also have *that* place where we escape. For some of us it's sitting on sugary white sand in front of a sea of turquoise. For others, it may be standing on the edge of a mountaintop surrounded by a forest of trees while staring out over the hills. Whatever the scene, we've all been there. Now would be a great time to take a minute and think of the place you call your own. Some people may choose to escape inside, but let's focus on the freedom of the great outdoors for a while. Picture the setting of that place where you get lost in God's creation. Close your eyes for a second, and surround yourself in this setting. Simply BE there…

Now I want to ask a question. Why? Why is *that* place *your* place? Why are we wired to find ourselves intoxicated by the beauty of nature? Chances are, your answer sounds something like, "It's peaceful," "I can think more clearly," or "To find rest." Again, I will ask. Why? Why do you think it is so peaceful? Why do you tend to "find" yourself when you are lost in nature?

It comes so natural for us to enjoy settings like the one I described earlier. In other words, it is in our nature to be in awe of nature. It is secretly innate in all of us. Even a recluse can't deny the beauty of a clear, night sky coated with millions of twinkling stars that were perfectly placed. My friends, it is not by accident or coincidence that we are drawn to adore the sights of this world.

THE SOURCE

Something happens in our brains when we are impressed with something. For some reason, we do not simply observe without pondering further. There is an extremely talented baker who has his own reality show because of one reason. He creates the most unique and outstanding cakes. They are so spectacular, he got his own show so the world can see what he can do. If you have ever seen this show, you see the finished portrait of a cake and become fascinated, but in your heads, it does not end there. Something else happens. We automatically start thinking, "How did he do that? Could I do that?" It goes through our heads every time. Think of a masterpiece of a painting, a young child who sings in a way that brings you to tears, or a building that seems more than just a building when you walk inside because of how majestically crafted it is. We always seem to wonder…How?

Think of the wonders of the world. Why are they called the *wonders* of the world? It is because the things we are most impressed by make us wonder how such things exist. We know that there is no chance we could ever build or create such a creation, so we wonder how the heck someone else did. How did he get the idea for that cake? How did that artist come up with that picture? How did that little girl get a voice like that? How did that architect envision a building so beautiful? It also happens that the more impressed we are with something, the more we tend to find ourselves in a state of wonder or curiosity. We are intrigued and drawn in. Although we find ourselves full of wonder about the creation or thing we seemed to be impressed with, it is amazing to me how we never seem to question the existence of the source. You never fall in love with a painting and ask yourself if there was an artist. When your child brings home the masterpiece of a clay pot they made at school, you don't question who made the clay pot. You already know who made it. You have proof. When you walk into that building that captures your focus, do you find yourself wondering if someone actually built it? No.

There are a couple of very important things these creations do for their creators. One result is that the creations prove the existence of the creators. The other thing that happens is that the creations glorify the creators. The ability, performance, and the piece of art all do a fantastic job of showing off what the creator can do. We rarely question if there *was* a creator and more commonly become more curious *about* the creator. Again, this is not by accident.

    Let's get back to nature. Think of the mountains, oceans, trees, flowers, stars, forests, meadows, etc. All of these things are real and tangible for us to see. Another thing they have in common is that they are all creations. As a review, what two things do creations do? Prove a creator and glorify the creator. Let's treat these creations just like the other creations I mentioned earlier. We don't question if a creator exists. We simply ponder how it happened. This is true with every human on the planet. We stare out into space, across miles of hills, and observe every created thing visible to us, and we never once question *if* it was created. The visible qualities of what we are looking at proves that it, in fact, was created and that there was a creator. I'm sitting in a Starbucks at the moment, and I do not question someone built this building. I have never met the builder, I don't know the builder, but that does not change the fact that I know the builder exists. How do I know? The evidence. I'm sitting in a chair looking at what he or she built. I am experiencing what they created at this very moment. Knowing everything about the creator is not a prerequisite for realizing there is one.

NO EXCUSES

I have been around many people who express the need for Christians to reach people who have never heard the gospel. I completely agree, by the way. It is what Jesus commanded of Christians. "Go and make disciples of all nations..." I get that part. One thing Christians seem to always assume, however, is that these people (the ones who have never been to church, met God, talked to God, or even heard of God) have no idea that there is a creator. These people may not know the Creator, but they are fully provided with evidence that there is one. I am surely not trying to sound insensitive about this topic of reaching the unreached. All I'm trying to do is point out that God created this universe and everything in it to reveal His existence and His glory. Paul actually writes to the Romans and brings up the point of every human on the planet being provided with evidence of a creator.

"For ever since the world was created, people have seen the earth and sky. Through everything God made, they can clearly see his invisible qualities—his eternal power and divine nature. So they have no excuse for not knowing God."
Romans 1:20 (New Living Translation)

I know this sounds harsh. It never tickles when someone says, "You have no excuse." This is a very revealing sentence, though, and it brings a lot of truth and clarification to us about why God created all that He did. God's character is constantly being exposed through the tangible qualities of all that He created, especially nature. I have never met Pablo Picasso, but his paintings show me a glimpse of his character. He is unique, he sees things differently, he goes against the grain, he is creative, and he is willing to take chances. People were impressed with his creations even without fully understanding the artist. They can, however, understand what he is trying to communicate through his paintings. His creations were his fingerprints, and they made him one of the most famous artists to ever live. It is no different with God. He is speaking to us and showing Himself to us through His creations. Every sunrise, sunset, and glorious picture of nature is God screaming, "I am awesome! I am beautiful! I am big! I know what gets your attention! I am powerful, and I am in control! You can trust me! I am full of glory! Look what I can do!"

SPEECHLESS

One of my favorite books in the Bible is the book of Job. Job had everything and was extremely blessed by God. God then allowed everything to be taken away from him. Then, God allowed Job to become physically ill. Job tried to keep his faith but eventually, his faith began to bend as his life continued to fall apart. This leads Job to question God's faithfulness. In doing so, Job lodged himself between a rock and a hard place with God, and God does not hesitate to remind Job of His character. Please do me a favor and set this book aside to go read Job 38-42.

How does God challenge Job? He reminds him of everything He has created bringing up so many aspects of nature that show how powerful He really is. Have you ever found yourself wondering if God really exists? If God loves me, why doesn't He show more of Himself to me? If you have ever asks these things, put yourself in Job's shoes when God is speaking to him. Can you make the sun rise and set? Do the oceans and clouds obey your command? Did you equip the lion with his roar? Here's a challenge. Take a walk outside on a clear night and look up to the stars. Find a spot in the sky where one is missing, and open your mouth as if you wanted to place one in that exact spot. Chances are, you'll find yourself feeling a bit inadequate.

God can do what we cannot, and this is good because it brings us to a state of wonder. How did He do that? The thing about being curious is that we want to know more about what it is we are curious about. It draws us in, and we end up passing through a state of curiosity and rushing into an adoring state of awe. Our God is an awesome God. I love this conversation between God and Job because God very easily puts things back into perspective, and I love how He uses nature to accomplish that. Nature is constantly exposing who God is and what He can do. The Bible is flooded with passages where God is making a point using an aspect of nature. These are just a few examples, but take some time and look for your self:

> *"But ask the beasts, and they will teach you; the birds of the heavens, and they will tell you; or the bushes of the earth, and they will teach you; and the fish of the sea will declare to you. Who among all these does not know that the hand of the LORD has done this?"*

Job 12:7-9 (ESV)

> *"You are the LORD, you alone. You have made heaven, the heaven of heavens, with all their host, the earth and all that is on it, the seas and all that is in them; and you preserve all of them; and the host of heaven worships you.*
>
> Nehemiah 9:6 (ESV)

For since the creation of the world God's invisible qualities—his eternal power and divine nature—have been clearly seen, being understood from what has been made, so that people are without excuse.

Romans 1:20 (NIV)

For in him all things were created: things in heaven and on earth, visible and invisible,

whether thrones or powers or rulers or authorities; all things have been created through him and for him. ¹⁷ He is before all things, and in him all things hold together.
Colossians 1:16,17 (NIV)

For the LORD is God,
  and he created the heavens and earth
  and put everything in place.
He made the world to be lived in,
  not to be a place of empty chaos.
"I am the LORD," he says,
  "and there is no other.

Isaiah 45:18 (NLT)

When I look at your heavens, the work of your fingers,
  the moon and the stars, which you have set in place,
  what is man that you are mindful of him,
  and the son of man that you care for him?
Yet you have made him a little lower than the heavenly beings and crowned him with glory and honor.
You have given him dominion over the works of your hands;

you have put all things under his feet,
all sheep and oxen,
and also the beasts of the field,
the birds of the heavens, and the fish of the sea,
whatever passes along the paths of the seas.
O LORD, our Lord,
how majestic is your name in all the earth!

Psalm 8:3-9 (ESV)

What do all these verses show? God actually wants to reveal Himself to us. In creating the universe, God purposefully left His fingerprints on everything. Creations do two things. Prove there is a creator and glorify the creator. When you find yourself laying in a hammock and staring out over hills of endless trees in a state of adoration, two things are happening. God is revealing His work to you, and He is ultimately being glorified. When you consciously adore His work, you are inwardly saying in awe, "Hallowed by your name." God is most glorified by the redemption of His people. Every time we stand speechless in adoration over His beautiful creation, we are redeemed into His presence.

FOLLOW THE LEADER

I know a lot of people who claim that it is hard for them to connect with God. They say they feel as though their prayers don't go past the ceiling or as if God is simply not listening. They also claim that it is hard to see God working in their lives. They are trying and trying but simply cannot see Him. We know He is the creator, He is all-powerful, He is rich in love, and He is above everything and in control, but sometimes, we simply find it hard to connect with Him. I get it. It's understandable. His ways are not our ways, and He is very different than we are. Although we know this to be true, He really does want to connect with you. He wants the best for you, and He knows what's best for you is Him! He wants you to connect with Him and to see Him. The only problem is that this is sometimes the hardest part of following Him, the connection.

  I cannot wait to get to the chapter about Jesus later on in this book, but let's take a tiny look at Him for a moment. Jesus was fully God, but He was also fully human. If He were not fully human, He would not be able to fully relate to us. When Jesus lived His human life, He was setting the example for how we should live. Hence the trendy question, "What would Jesus do?" You were a big deal when you wore a bracelet with WWJD on it because it showed that you were trying to live a life that looked a lot like the one Jesus did. Here is some food for thought. If Jesus set the example for how we should do things, shouldn't we look at what He did for answers to our "how to" questions? Here's our predicament: How can we connect to God better and experience His presence in a real way? Now, let's look at what Jesus did.

Go through the Bible and look for instances where Jesus experienced God's presence in a fascinating way. I'll guide us through some examples. Jesus fasted for forty days and was tempted by the craftiest of deceivers (Matthew 4). The cool thing about this experience was that He leaned on His Father for a way out. He was able to overcome the enemy as the Father and Son defeated Satan together. In another instance, Jesus did what no other human could do by walking on water (John 6). This is significant because He was showing His disciples that if you had enough faith in God, anything would be possible. At another time in His ministry, Jesus took three of His closest friends to a special place for a supernatural meeting (Matthew 17). His three followers saw Jesus in a way they never had before and actually heard the voice of God from a cloud. Not long before Jesus was handed over, there was another special time between Him and His Father. He was spending some last special moments pleading and gaining strength from God. He asked God to let His wrath be taken away from Him, but He knew what had to be done (Matthew 26). Jesus could not have done what He did without the help from His Father.

Again, these are just a few examples from Jesus' life, but let's take a look at these four instances. What do they all have in common? God did something really cool, and Jesus was able to connect with God in a way we all long for. Something else, however, is quite significant in every scene. There is a little detail that is, in actuality, a big deal when it comes to each of these situations. We pass over it a lot when reading the Bible and take it for granted when talking about Jesus' ministry. Look closely at the setting. Look at where Jesus was most of the time when something supernatural happened. In all of these examples, Jesus was out in nature. When He was fasting and overcoming the temptation of Satan, He was out in the desert and wilderness. When He was showing His disciples how to have faith, He was out in the middle of the ocean. When He allowed His closest friends to meet with Him and experience God in a way they never have before, He took them on top of a mountain. When He was spending His last precious moments gaining strength and spending intimate time with His Father, He went into a garden.

Jesus was able to connect with God and experience Him in a real and tangible way just like

He wants us to do. He was able to do this by getting out and experiencing what God created for Him to experience. Everything in all creation was created by Him and for Him (Colossians 1:16). If everything belongs to God, shouldn't everything we experience bring us closer to God? He created everything for a purpose, and His purpose in creating every beautiful and majestic thing in nature was to build a playground for us to experience to bring us closer to Him. God is trying to connect with us and reveal Himself to us by showing us the gift of what He created. The only problem is that we are begging to see more of God but refusing to open our eyes and look at Him. Experiencing the creation helps us to experience the Creator. Jesus connected with God by spending time with Him in nature, so if we want to connect with God the way Jesus did, we should probably do what Jesus did.

THE CHALLENGE

I am not saying that we cannot spend time with God inside and get something incredible out of it. God can reveal Himself to you however He wants to reveal Himself to you. It is good for you to have a secret place where you and God can meet daily. Mine is in a specific chair in my office, and

God and I have had many intimate conversations in that place. I am speaking to those who are finding it hard to connect with God at all! If you are feeling as if your prayers are not going past the ceiling, go to a place where there is no ceiling. Go to where no human can block your site of what God created for you to see. Get out and stare off into space and fill your mind with great wonder. Too often, we tend to go through life with our blinds closed. Usually, we close our blinds because we don't want people to see inside. What we are also doing in the process is hindering our ability to see what is outside. We are missing something remarkable.

Let me give an example. I grew up in Atlanta about twenty minutes away from Stone Mountain. For those of you who don't know, Stone Mountain is the largest piece of exposed granite in the world and is a pretty awesome site to see. I spent a lot of my childhood going to that park, climbing the mountain, running the trails, watching the laser show, and enjoying the atmosphere. It finally got to a point, though, where I became *used* to it all. I would sit on the lawn in the summer watching the laser show on the face of the mountain and practically get to a state of boredom because I had seen it so many times. I remember sitting there one night watching the show, and all I remember hearing was a voice behind me repeating over and over, "Wow! That's awesome! Spectacular! Amazing!" Here I was becoming bored with what was going on while the person behind me was being blown away with what they were experiencing. This pattern occurs the same way for all of us when it comes to what God has created. We look outside at the trees and the sun giving us light to see. We walk in the night under a flawless array of shining stars. We are going through life and glancing at nature in a state of boredom without realizing what it is we are actually seeing.

We have the opportunity to see God, through faith, every time we walk out the door. Every commute to work, every sunrise and sunset, every season that comes along, every time you go for a jog, every walk to the mailbox...Your day is full of opportunities to be in awe of the one and only Creator. My challenge to you is to take advantage of those opportunities. We are claiming that we do not see God, but it is hard to see with your eyes closed. When you find yourself in a state of awe and wonder and adoring the universe He created for you to adore, you can find yourself in the presence of God. All that He created shows us who He is, and every second we experience His creation is a second more that He is glorified.

Chapter 6

Gone Fishing
It may take some fishing for men to see God.

The greatest gift my father ever gave me was teaching me how to trout fish. Every time I think of spending time with my dad and my brother together, I can't help but picture myself on the bank of a north Georgia river with the sight of them casting out their lines downstream. For each of us, it is our third love behind Jesus and our wives. If you're a man in the Cook family, it is in your blood to be a fisherman. I'll never forget my father and my brother being at my wedding. My dad gave his speech at our rehearsal dinner, and his inspiring words pointed directly to the well-known phrase, "If you give a man a fish, you'll feed him for a day; if you teach a man to fish, you'll feed him for a lifetime." It is as if those wise words were created just for him to use on that night. I'll always remember my brother, who was one of my best men, coming up to me and admitting that my father actually said exactly what he was going to say in his speech. I felt bad for my brother, but it couldn't have been more perfect at the same time. Instead of taking away from what my brother was going to say, in my head, all I can hear is both of their voices together. I would have shared the same statement if the situation were reversed. We all felt the same way about fishing for those rainbow trout.

My Father, my brother, and I have not always perfectly understood each other. It's not that we did not get along; we all just had our own thing going on. I can't think of many times where we all sat together and had a heart-to-heart. One thing about the Cook boys, however, is that we all share a love for trout fishing. We may all be at different places in our lives, but when we step out of that truck with waders on and poles ready, we all carry the same heartbeat. We head down the trails toward the stream with the same goals and aspirations, the same love and determination. If anything was ever misunderstood between us, that all changed once we casted our lines. I love both of them dearly and can't have a thought about fishing without them coming to mind. There's a famous Thomas Kinkaid painting that is titled *Almost Heaven*. I love the painting because it is of a fisherman out in the wilderness standing right in the middle of a river tossing out his line. It is a perfect sight and brings total tranquility when I look at it. The only thing missing in the painting, in my mind, is two more gentlemen fishing downstream.

With all that being said, fishing is a big part of my life. There is so much more to those words in that wise sentence, "If you teach a man to fish, you feed him for a lifetime." What all three of us have realized over the years is that we got so much more out of trout fishing than a free meal whenever we wanted one. Growing up on the trout stream taught me so much about life that I could easily write another book simply on this topic alone. We'll see how this one goes first. As you can probably tell at this point, I am not simply one who notices things without going a bit deeper. It is no different with the topic of fishing. The joy that fills my heart every time I make the trip to the Chattahoochee National Forest does not stem from simply catching a few fish. My satisfaction does not lie in the result of how successful I am at the end of the day. There is so much more to it than the fish.

It's about getting away from the distractions of the world and all the noise. It's about stepping out of the truck and breathing in the cold air with nothing but the sound of a running stream in the background. It's about seeking something out that takes effort. It's about spending time thoroughly enjoying everything God created for me to enjoy (referring to the chapter about nature). It's about whispering to God how great of a job He did creating it all as the fog from my breath fills the air.

I could go on and on with everything I love about trout fishing, but I think you are starting to get the idea. Looking back over the years, it has become clear to me how God was revealing Himself to me through my adventures on the river. There are so many things about fishing that relate to my walk with Christ, but again, I will save all that for later. The goal of this chapter is to reveal God in a way that we possibly have never seen Him before, through the idea of fishing.

RECRUITING

One of the things about Jesus' life I find quite fascinating is how he selected his first followers. In Matthew 4, Jesus said these words,

> *"Come, follow me, and I will make you fishers of men."*
>
> Matthew 4:19 (NIV)

He's walking along the Sea of Galilee, and all of a sudden, He sees two men fishing in a boat. He calls out to them with the command we just looked at, and that's it. They drop their nets and everything they are doing to follow Him. I really want to look at what Jesus promises these two men. I think it is something we skim over a lot when He uses *those* words for *those* men. He told these *fishermen* that He would make them fishers *of* men. Whether you are a Christian or not, I think we can all agree that when it comes to God, things just don't happen by chance. I find it hard to believe that Jesus was just walking along and simply chose the first two people He saw. I think Jesus was being very intentional in where He was walking and whom He was going to give this command to. I have not taken enough theological history classes to fully back this up, but I do have a theory as to why Jesus chose these two men as His first disciples. They were fishermen. They did this for a living, which means they were probably good at it. Humor me for a second, but maybe Jesus, quite possibly, might have chosen these specific men because they were good at catching things. This was not simply a recreational activity for them. Providing for their families, having food to eat, and bringing in an income were all dependent on these men catching what they were fishing for. Peter and Andrew had probably been fishing for most of their lives, which equipped them with a very specific set of skills.

I have also grown up fishing throughout my life, so I understand what skills are needed to be a successful fisherman. To catch what you are seeking, it takes a lot of preparation. You need to know what equipment you need, where you are going, what kind of bait you are going to use, what specific kind of fish you are fishing for, when the right time of day to fish is, and a knowledge of specifically knowing where the fish are and what they are attracted to. Along with preparation skills, there are personal traits that are needed to get the job done. Some of these traits include patience, perseverance, creativity, and boldness. Patience is needed because fish are not always predictable. Sometimes it takes time. I can remember being a child and not catching a lot of fish because... well, I was a child. What do children do? They move and squirm and don't like to stay still for long periods of time. A great fisherman needs to be patient.

Perseverance is needed because some days are worse than others. Fishermen cannot quit because they had a bad day fishing. One thing I had to learn growing up was that there are days the fish bite, and there are days that they don't. No child likes to go home empty-handed when they've been trying to catch something all day. It took going back over and over again to realize that, although I might not catch something one day, my nets would be overflowing the next day. Great fishermen can persevere.

Creativity is needed because what you are using to catch the fish may not always work. As I stated earlier, fish are not always predictable. You could go out one day fishing with a particular type of bait and catch nothing. Then you see another fisherman walking by with a stringer full of fish. I've been blessed enough to be on the other end of the deal more times than not. I'll be walking back towards the truck with my limit of fish caught, and someone with nothing to show for their work will come up and ask, "What kind of bait are you using?" Most of the time, the bait I use works, but sometimes, it doesn't. When it's not working, I don't pack up my stuff and leave thinking the fish singled me out. I keep fishing, and I try something else knowing, sooner or later, I'll find something they'll bite. Great fishermen have to set aside their pride sometimes and be creative.

Finally, every fisherman needs a pinch of boldness. Fishing is seeking. You have to be willing to go where no one else will go and try what no one else will try to catch what no one else has caught. I remember one specific time going trout fishing when I was in college. My buddy, Jonathan, and I just got up to the campground when a guy came up to us and said, "You might as well pack everything back up and leave because we've been up here all weekend and haven't got a single bite." Talk about a buzz killer. We could have listened to him and left, but we decided to go anyway. We woke up at 6 in the morning with it raining and just warm enough to keep the rain from freezing. It was miserable. We went anyway. I remember looking down at the stream and seeing a specific hole I wanted to fish in. Again, another gentleman walked by and said, "No need to go down there. I've been fishing for about an hour and have gotten nothing." It may sound like I sacrificed some wisdom and that I don't listen to advice much, but I went anyway. I got down to the bend of the river and cast my line just in the wake behind a large rock. Within seconds, I had him. I say him, but I have no idea how to tell the gender of a fish. It felt like a normal fish, but when I stuck my net down to pick it up, I was amazed. This was the biggest trout I had ever caught in my life. We didn't catch a single fish after that one, but it was enough to feed and satisfy both of us for dinner. I was blessed with that fish because I was willing to try what no one else would try despite what people were telling me. Great fishermen must have a boldness that leads them to trying new things.

If Peter and Andrew were professional fishermen, they probably had all of these skills. Maybe Jesus was not necessarily looking for two random guys on a boat. Maybe Jesus was looking for a particular set of skills, a set of skills that enabled these men to be great at catching what they were fishing for. Maybe Jesus had a plan to go fishing and wanted to use followers who knew what it took to be great fishermen. Maybe Jesus knew it was going to take great fishermen to create great fishers of men.

LEARNING FROM THE MASTER

As I mentioned earlier in the chapter, everything I learned about catching fish, I learned from my dad. It took many years and many fishing trips to get to where I am today. There is no other way around it. Most of what I have learned about catching fish was not taught in lecture form. It came through observation and demonstration. Every time we got on the river, my eyes were on two things, my line and my dad. I would just watch him sometimes seeing exactly where he tossed the bait, how long he waited to reel after getting a bite, and how he kept the fish on the hook. My knowledge has come from years and years of seeing him set the example. I would watch him, and I would try to copy it. I was smart enough to know it worked because of the fish he caught, so why not copy it? From picking out a fishing hole, to getting the hook out of the fish to cleaning the fish, I observed and copied and copied and copied. My father, brother, and I don't live quite as close anymore, so I have taken many trips over the past several years on my own. The tranquility I receive on the river has remained the same, but my skill and ability has grown to a new level. I'm not trying to sound arrogant, but when you practice something over and over again, you're bound to pick it up pretty well. And to be honest, isn't that the point? I mentioned my friend, Jonathan, earlier who is my new fishing partner. He's a great fisherman and one of my favorite people, but I'd like to say I've taught him a few things when it comes to fishing. I'm sure he'll get a kick out of this. I love every second of it though. I thoroughly enjoy sharing the knowledge I have received from watching my dad and through personal experience. My dad gave me the gift of teaching me how to fish. The reward is knowing I will never have to go hungry. My favorite part of gaining that knowledge, however, has been the joy of sharing it. It would be completely selfish of me to not share what I have graciously been given. What's so crazy about it, though, is that every time I pass on a little bit of what I know, I feel a little bit closer to my dad. Are you starting to see the picture?

Jesus came into the world for two distinct reasons: to seek out those who were lost and to save them (Luke 19:10). In a way, Jesus came into the world as a master fisherman. He came with every bit of knowledge he needed to catch what he came into this world to catch. He had every bit of preparation, patience, perseverance, creativity, and boldness that was needed to get the job done. A fisherman would be a lot more successful if he knew everything about the fish, knew exactly what the fish was thinking, and knew exactly what the fish was going to do next. Jesus had this part down. He knew His people better than they knew themselves, He knew everything they thought, and He knew exactly what was going to happen next.

Just as we saw a little earlier, Jesus grabbed some fishermen. Since He knew what was going to happen to Him, He knew that He was going to need a little company to pass on His knowledge. So Jesus calls out to these fishermen, grabs a couple more in James and John, and it is so bizarre what happens next. Look in your Bible at Matthew 4. I'm going to look at two verses back to back here starting in verse 22:

> *²² and immediately they left the boat and their father and followed him. ²³ Jesus went throughout Galilee, teaching in their synagogues, proclaiming the good news of the kingdom, and healing every disease and sickness among the people.*
>
> Matthew 4:22-23 (NIV)

Did you catch that? They followed Him… and He began teaching and proclaiming the good news. He doesn't take them off to a retreat somewhere or have them sign up for a 9-week course. He calls them to follow Him, and He begins teaching. He comes into the world as a fisherman, grabs a few more fishermen, and immediately begins to fish. Right after it says Jesus begins teaching and healing throughout Galilee, He gives the Sermon on the Mount. This fisherman is not wasting any time. Jesus was not holding these separate lectures for His disciples at this point. He just wanted them with Him to watch Him, to see every move He made. He wanted them to learn from Him simply by being with Him. They got to observe every word Jesus spoke, how He said it, and who specifically He said it to. It was as if Jesus told a few guys on the side of the road to follow Him, grabbed His waders, went into the river, and just started showing off His fishing skills. The way I surveyed every move my dad made in the river when I was a boy is how I picture these first disciples staring in awe at what Jesus was doing. He recruited them for a reason and immediately began training them without them even noticing. He was preparing them for the future. He knew what was going to happen and needed them to see how true fishing was done. Jesus knew there would be a day when He would give them the great commission to go into all the world and make disciples and do what He had been doing the whole time (Matthew 28:19). All He wanted from them at this point, however, was to watch. Later they would have the opportunity to copy.

YOU'RE A NATURAL

You may be reading this and finding it very hard to connect with what I'm talking about. Maybe your view of fishing is being lazy in a boat out in the middle of a lake. You may have never even held a fishing pole, much less used one to catch fish. Maybe you wouldn't even know where to start if someone gave you all that you needed to catch something and told you good luck. You could be a master fisherman, or you could be someone whose never step foot in a boat or on a riverbank. Whatever your skill or experience level is, take heart because there is actually a true fisherman in all of us. To some of you that is a compliment, and you're welcome. To others that is an insult, in which case I plead, let me explain.

There was a time in my life when I was in high school. I was one of the captains on the football team, made good grades, had lots of friends, and I had one thing on my mind...finding the perfect girl. Every guy has this on their mind at some point in their lives. All the guys who just read that said a big, "Yup!" in their heads. Now I'm a little old-fashioned, and I fully believe that it is the man's responsibility to pursue the girl. Most every woman loves to be pursued, and almost every guy loves a good chase. Let's think about what a guy is doing when he is "pursuing" a girl. I'll share my brief knowledge of what a smart guy does. He is patient and takes his time. He finds out who she hangs out with and what her interests are. He talks to her friends and tries to discover what makes her happy or what gets her heart beating. I feel like I'm giving the other team all of our plays…sorry guys! Once he has all the needed information, he cleans himself up and makes his move simply hoping and praying that she'll "take the bait." What is he doing when he is pursuing? He's fishing. He has prepared as much as he can, he knows he's fishing in the right spot, but like we've already discussed, sometimes the fish are unpredictable. That's where the praying comes in. Where do you think they get the line, "There are lots of fish in the sea?" When we are pursuing a relationship, we are fishing and hoping to get a bite.

Now let's talk about the ladies. You try fishing in a completely different way, but you are still fisherwomen nonetheless. Let me give you a scene. Guy and girl are about to go out on a romantic date. Guy spends about twenty minutes getting ready. Not so with girl. Girl's whole day is planned around the time she needs to get all did up. She could spend about two to three hours getting ready depending on where they are in the relationship. Guy picks up girl, and they go to a fancy restaurant. Guy and girl are sitting there when another girl walks by. Guy's girl says, "Wow, she's like so pretty." Guy has to be very careful because this is not just an observatory comment. This is a test. The right answer is for guy to object, "She doesn't hold a candle to you, sweetheart." All the women who just read that said a big "Yup!" in their heads. What is the girl doing when she declares something like that? She's fishing! It happens all the time. Women always say stuff like, "I'm fat, I don't feel pretty, or I hate my hair," and that is their bait. They are waiting for us guys to bite by taking the bait and re-affirming how much they mean to us. This is defined as "fishing for compliments." Men and women both know how to fish.

Maybe you aren't into the whole dating thing and still have no idea what I'm talking about. We go fishing every time we throw ourselves out their simply hoping someone will take the bait. Think about a job interview. You walk in with your résumé longing for the interviewer to take the bait. I remember when I was about to interview for teaching jobs. So many professors and advisors were equipping me with what to wear, what to say, how to present your self as a professional, and so on. You are wanting to impress whoever is interviewing you, so you prepare by finding out what they like, what they chase, how to approach them, etc. All of these things are bait. You are a fisherman looking for a job, so you go fishing.

We are all natural fishermen (and fisherwomen) when you get down to it. Whether you like it or not, you're a fisherman. We've all been fishing in our lives whether it is on the bank of a river or sitting in a romantic restaurant. If you are one of those who were insulted by the fact of being called a fisherman, take heart. Jesus showed Himself to be quite fond of fishermen.

FISHING WITH A PURPOSE

One pastor and author once proclaimed a very wise truth. He said, "When purpose is unknown, abuse is inevitable." What an incredible thought. There is a purpose for everything. It's easy for us to think of some examples in today's world that exemplify this truth. Take drugs, for example.

A drug's purpose is to bring us back to health when we are sick or injured. When the purpose of a drug is unknown, abuse is inevitable. Think of guns, knives, and relationships. If they are not used according to their original purpose, abuse occurs.

I'm not going to go too deep into this at the moment, but as we know, God created everything. He created it all and said that it was GOOD. Everything he created was good, and everything revealed so much of His glory. Then sin came into the picture and distorted what God originally created. It turned sex from a permanent union of two people into a selfish and temporary pleasure. It turned a gracious resource of money into something that takes control of our lives. When purpose is unknown, abuse is inevitable.

As I confidently stated before, I think Jesus was very intentional in choosing fishermen as his first disciples. We've seen that we have all been fishing. Some of us have even become really great at it. Here's some food for thought. What if we used our ability to fish for its original purpose? What if there is a reason some of us are so good at understanding what the fish are thinking and how to catch them? Maybe God gave you that specific set of skills for a greater purpose than what you've been using them for. There are probably guys out there "fishing" that are going to enjoy the thrill of catching the fish only to release it not knowing that beautiful fish is just going to float to the top once they throw it back in. When purpose is unknown, abuse is inevitable.

One of the last things Jesus commanded of His disciples was to go and make disciples of all nations (Matthew 28:19). In terms of the topic we have been talking about, He told these fishermen to go fishing the way He had taught them to fish. They had a particular set of skills for a reason, and that reason was so much more than having an animal bite a rusty hook. Those disciples were given a gift of knowing how to fish, and Jesus was calling them to share it. Jesus said to go and make disciples. Don't just go out giving people some fish. Go teach them *how* to fish. In doing so, you are not just giving them the satisfaction of a full stomach, you are showing them they way to the ultimate satisfaction so they will never have to go hungry again.

What if we took our abilities and our particular set of fishing skills and reprogramed them? If you aren't getting the point yet, you are great at fishing because God wants you to go fishing for souls. He wants you to do what Jesus did and seek the lost. Some of you are great with people. You understand people, you're a great listener, people seem to connect with you, and it comes natural for you to draw people in. My friends, you were given this ability for a purpose. When we use our gift of fishing by making disciples, we are using our gift for its original purpose. When this happens, God is clearly seen, and He is glorified.

WE NEED HELP

I know we are all getting excited and can't wait to use our fishing skills to go tell people they smell like fish and Jesus wants us to hook them and all that jazz, but we must understand something very important before we "go." The bad news is that you can't go by yourself. The good news is that you have complete access to the help you need.

When I was a child, I needed help from my father. I saw water and got so excited that I just threw my bait in the water expecting to pull out the catch of the day every time. Here's the problem. I had no idea what I was doing. Some of you may be feeling the same way. "Alright, I am willing to go fishing for souls, but where do I start and what do I say?"

I stood close to my dad when I was fishing as a boy because I needed his guidance. I needed him with me to be successful. I remember he would advise, "Joseph, throw it right over there in between those two rocks. That's where the fish are. Joseph, wait for the fish to bite a couple times before you start reeling in. Joseph, you have to be patient. Leave the bait in the water a little longer or else the fish won't have the opportunity to bite it."

I went fishing a couple months ago for my birthday just before the end of trout season. My friend, Jonathan, was with me, and we were standing on the riverbank near a hole that looked promising. He fished with me for a bit but had no luck, so he decided to walk downstream to try somewhere else. I looked out across the stream right in front of where he was previously standing, and my dad's voice rang clear in my head. "Joseph, see that log in the water over there? Toss your line just at the trunk and let the bait float down under the log. That's where the fish are." Sure enough, I cast my line and caught four trout in that exact spot. Two of those trout were even bigger than the fish I earlier described as the biggest fish I had ever caught. They were monsters!

There's a similar story in the Bible. It's actually pretty interesting how all this works out. When Jesus started his ministry, His disciples were fishing when He first called out to them. Now, we fast-forward to after Jesus died and rose from the dead. He's bringing His ministry on Earth to a close and shows us a very similar situation. Most of His disciples had not seen Him alive yet, and they were all together so decided to go fishing. Let's take a look.

> *³ "I'm going out to fish," Simon Peter told them, and they said, "We'll go with you." So they went out and got into the boat, but that night they caught nothing.*
>
> *⁴ Early in the morning, Jesus stood on the shore, but the disciples did not realize that it was Jesus.*
>
> *⁵ He called out to them, "Friends, haven't you any fish?"*

"No," they answered.

⁶ He said, "Throw your net on the right side of the boat and you will find some." When they did, they were unable to haul the net in because of the large number of fish.
John 21:3-6 (NIV)

    I love this story! The disciples have been fishing all night and have nothing to show for it. They tried everything they could, but the fish simply would not bite. Then comes Jesus as He says, "Throw your net on the right side of the boat. That's where the fish are." Sure enough, they follow the orders as their wish is finally granted. They couldn't even haul the fish in because there were so many. This story always reminds me of my father showing me where the fish were when I was a child. With the help of our guides, the disciples and I finally were able to catch what we were fishing for. Without God's help, we will always come up empty-handed.

    Here in the twenty-first century, it is clear that we don't have the convenient access of Jesus just showing up on the shore to show us where to go or what to say. Jesus is no longer here, but that doesn't mean we are on our own. On the contrary, Jesus actually tells us that we will always have complete access to Him.

> *"And surely I am with you always, to the very end of the age."*
>
> Matthew 28:20b (NIV)

God was the creator of everything. To pay for our sins, God turned Himself into a human named Jesus. Jesus died on the cross, rose back to life, and then ascended into heaven. Then, God graciously provided another way for us to have access to Him through the Holy Spirit. Jesus explained it a little better to His disciples when He was here. This is what He said.

> *"Nevertheless, I tell you the truth: it is to your advantage that I go away, for if I do not go away, the Helper will not come to you. But if I go, I will send him to you."*
>
> John 16:7 (ESV)

God was telling His disciples and us that, although He was going up to heaven and leaving us here on Earth, He was going to send Himself to us in the form of the Holy Spirit. I also love how the English Standard Version used the description "Helper." That is exactly what the Holy Spirit does. He helps us. He speaks to us. Just like how I heard my dad's voice telling me where to cast my line, God speaks to us through the power of the Holy Spirit. He is willing to show us where the fish are and what kind of bait to use. He is willing to show us who to talk to and what to say to them. Too many people are wasting their lives because they feel too inadequate to be used by God. We *are* inadequate, but with the help of the Helper, we have the ability to catch a load that is too heavy to haul in. God wants to use you! He is just waiting for you to pick up your pole. He wants you to go fishing. He wants you to go and make disciples of all nations. He'll show you where to go. He'll even show you what to say and how to say it.

Every time I take that trip up to the Chattahoochee National Forest and step into the river with my waders on and pole in my hand, I know my father is with me. He is not always physically there, but it is amazing how tangible he becomes when I hear his voice. If you haven't heard from God in a while and He seems a bit intangible, maybe He's waiting on you to pick up your pole and join Him in the river. We already know we're good at fishing. When we program that skill and use it for the purpose God intended by making disciples, His work in your life will become more real than you ever thought possible.

Chapter 7

Do You Believe In Miracles?
It may take a miracle to see God.

Living around Atlanta, one of the brilliant things Georgians get the joy of experiencing on a daily basis is traffic. Just reading or saying that word causes a lot of us to have to stop what we're doing and go to our "happy place." No matter what type of person is driving the car, we can all agree that sitting in traffic is not exactly the ideal way to spend your day. It is frustrating and gets our blood pressure climbing. The reason traffic can be frustrating is because we all have places to be, and we want to get there on time. I can remember so many times when I have been driving to somewhere important like a meeting or something and thinking specifically in my head, "It will be a miracle if I get there on time." I can recall saying it out loud a few times; my wife can vouch for that. Maybe you have thought those words or some variation of those words as well. "It will be a miracle if I get out of here alive. It will be a miracle if my parents don't ground me for life. It will be a miracle if I pass this exam. It will be a miracle if we win this game. It's a miracle he didn't burn the rolls."

We've all been there, simply yearning for a miracle. We've all been there because we are all living on the same planet and are all undergoing this little thing called life. Stuff happens. I'm not trying to sound pessimistic, but if we were being honest, I think we can all admit that, at some point in our lives, we have all fallen into a circumstance where the odds are completely against us. We have been caught between a rock and hard place and facing something we don't feel like we can face. We end up in a mess looking for a way out knowing full well there is no one around who can help. So we hope for a miracle. It's the only place left to put our hope.

Since we have all been in similar positions, we can all agree on our view of a miracle. For most of us, it is kind of hard to describe exactly what a miracle is, but what we *do* know is that we like them. Miracles are good. Why else would we hope for them? Nobody would object to having something miraculous happen in their life. We all want to experience good things. We are all in need of a miracle, and we have no problem asking for one. Unfortunately, we have gotten to a point where we don't really comprehend what it is we are actually asking for. There is a certain mystery behind a miracle that has become invisible to us; a power that we have gotten too tired to chase. The goal of this chapter is to unlock that mystery and reveal the true goodness that draws us to desire something miraculous in our lives.

WHAT MAKES A MIRACLE?

As I mentioned before, a miracle is something that is hard to describe. It is something beautiful and good and beneficial, but how can you define it? Who decides what constitutes a miracle and what doesn't? When preparing for this chapter, I did something so profound to get a solid answer for this question. I went out to a desert and spent a month in silence looking for a sign. No, that's crazy. I looked in the Merriam-Webster Dictionary app on my phone. Like I said…profound. You may be expecting some explanation of what the word "miracle" means in the Greek language or what culture it originated in, but that is not where I'm going. I want this chapter and these meanings to be as clear as possible because it is important that we understand the idea I am trying to convey. Here we go, a simple, English definition from a common dictionary.

Miracle- An extraordinary event manifesting divine intervention in human affairs.

Let's break that down. We get the extraordinary event part. We have already covered that. I really want to focus on the "manifesting divine intervention in human affairs" part. This is huge in revealing the tangibility of God.

As we saw in the chapter about nature, there was a time when God created everything that is visible and invisible. He created everything with a purpose. All that He created had a function, and He set it in motion. This is the exact reason why every living thing does what it does. Why does fire burn? God made it that way. Why does water make things wet? God made it that way. Why do we stay grounded to the Earth? Gravity holds us down… because God made it that way. Things happen the way they do because that is what was set in motion when everything was created. We describe this sometimes as, "the nature of the object." Fire burns because of the nature of fire. There is a logical reason for why you get burned when you get too physical with flames. God made it that way.

As we are here on Earth, we have a structure for everything. This is what is meant when the definition above mentions human affairs. There is a huge cause-and-effect relationship for everything that happens on this little blue planet. It is as if this is just how it is. Fire burns, water soaks, trees grow, and people die because that is life, and that is what is *supposed* to happen. What we do, our business as humans, is our human affairs. What we see in our given definition is that a miracle is when there is a manifested divine intervention in those human affairs. In simpler terms, miracles happen when a divine being intervenes on what is *supposed* to happen.

One of the greatest things about living in the neighborhood where I grew up was my group of friends. Every day I got home from school, I would throw my backpack in the house and race to where we all met up to play. We did it all. We played baseball, football, basketball, soccer, jumped on the trampoline, played hide and seek, etc. Along with these activities, we loved to create our own made-up games. We would install boundaries, goals, rules, and so on. The aspect we loved most about creating our own game was the fact that we could change the rules whenever we wanted. Others may have thought that the rules were not realistic or weird, but we had every right to change them because we were the ones who created them in the first place. The creator is usually the only one who has the authority to say what goes when it comes to the creation.

With that truth in mind, God created the rules of nature. He makes it very clear who all was present at the beginning.

> *"In the beginning, God created the heavens and the earth."*
>
> Genesis 1:1 (NIV)

In the beginning, God...that's it. God and God alone created it all without the help of anyone else. Since God is the only One who created the world we live in and how we live in it (human affairs), He is the only One who has the authority to intervene on those human affairs. A miracle is when God intervenes on what is supposed to logically happen. It is when nature says something is going to happen, but God intervenes with His plans. Why would He do that? If He created nature the way He wanted it, why would He intervene on what He already set in place? Because God desires to reveal even MORE of Himself to you and me through doing so.

There is a specific word in the definition of a miracle that we nonchalantly looked over. It is the word **manifested**. I found the English definition in the same dictionary as before, and I am going to repeat the definition of a miracle just as a review and to make my point.

Manifest- readily perceived by the senses and especially by the sense of sight.

Miracle- An extraordinary event manifesting divine intervention in human affairs.

This is incredible. In other words, **a miracle is when we actually see God interrupt human affairs by performing something extraordinary.** Something is supposed to happen, God does something only God can do, and we are able to witness it with our own eyes. That is why miracles are such a gift. This is what makes them so sweet, the ability to see God at work.

EXAMPLES FROM THE PAST

God has been revealing Himself through performing miracles ever since the creation of the world, which was a miracle on its own. My memory may be a little hazy, but I do not recall anyone else in history ever having the ability to speak light into existence. Think about it. God created everything out of nothing. He said for it to be, and it was. Period. One of the most famous miracles of all time is one people always think about when they think of God doing the impossible. Moses tells the story in the book of Exodus in chapter 14. The smell of freedom is still fresh for the Israelites, as God has just begun the process of deliverance. Pharaoh of Egypt just let them go, but God hardened his heart, which resulted in Pharaoh changing his mind. The Israelites are setting up camp right at the Red Sea when they witness the Egyptian army coming after them. The people began to panic, understandably, and started yelling at Moses for putting them in a bind. All the while God has a specific plan. I can just hear Him thinking, "I can't wait to see their faces in about 30 seconds." He provides the Israelites with a way of escape that was impossible for man to accomplish. Here is where we pick up:

> *²¹ Then Moses stretched out his hand over the sea, and all that night the LORD drove the sea back with a strong east wind and turned it into dry land. The waters were divided, ²² and the Israelites went through the sea on dry ground, with a wall of water on their right and on their left.*
>
> Exodus 14: 21-22 (NIV)

Most of us have heard this story before. We have heard about this God parting the Red Sea so His people could cross, but I want you to take a second and actually put yourself on the shore that night. Would you be able to believe what you were seeing? A huge wall of salty water on your left and another on the right as high as you could see with a perfect, dry path going straight through the center. Did you notice the word "dry?" As if it wasn't enough that there was a perfect part in the sea, God dries up the ground in an instant. This is not supposed to happen. Water is supposed to follow the rules of gravity, and it is definitely supposed to make whatever it touches wet. This is one extraordinary event where God did something miraculous, and all of His people were able to see it. God even tells us that that is exactly why He did it in the first place. A revealing verse prior to the ones we just looked at reflects God's intent in performing this miracle.

> *[18] The Egyptians will know that I am the LORD when I gain glory through Pharaoh, his chariots and his horsemen."*
> Exodus 14:18 (NIV)

Why does God allow the Israelites to go through on dry land, and have the water crash and swallow up the Egyptians? Why does He do this? He tells us that He does it so they will know exactly who He is and what He can do. He sets up this entire scene, this extraordinary event simply to reveal Himself in a more tangible way. Amazing.

A little later in history comes another story that you may have heard of. This story is one of my favorites and is found in the third chapter of the book of Daniel. It would be best for you to go ahead and read all of chapter 3, but I will briefly summarize it. There was a famous king named Nebuchadnezzar who was ruling over the land at the time. What a name, right? Nebuchadnezzar gets to a point where he is quite fond of himself and shows it by building a huge statue of himself. He then requires all of the people to bow down and worship the image he has created. He also informs them that whoever does not bow down and worship the image will be punished by being thrown into a fiery furnace. Sure enough, everyone bows down with the exception of three men named Shadrach, Meshach and Abednego. As a result, the king calls them to come into his presence and tries one more time. They still refuse to bow to him, so the king heats up the furnace as high as he can and has the three men thrown into the furnace. Now, I can't really speak from experience, but I think we can all agree what is *supposed* to happen when your body is totally consumed by fire. What should happen is actually exactly what happens to the guards that throw the men into the furnace. If you are thrown into flames of fire, you are supposed to burn. Again, I can see God saying, "Oh, this will be good." Let's see what happens:

> *²⁴ Then King Nebuchadnezzar leaped to his feet in amazement and asked his advisers, "Weren't there three men that we tied up and threw into the fire?" They replied, "Certainly, Your Majesty." ²⁵ He said, "Look! I see four men walking around in the*

fire, unbound and unharmed, and the fourth looks like a son of the gods." [26] Nebuchadnezzar then approached the opening of the blazing furnace and shouted, "Shadrach, Meshach and Abednego, servants of the Most High God, come out! Come here!" So Shadrach, Meshach and Abednego came out of the fire, [27] and the satraps, prefects, governors and royal advisers crowded around them. They saw that the fire had not harmed their bodies, nor was a hair of their heads singed; their robes were not scorched, and there was no smell of fire on them.

Daniel 3:24-27 (NIV)

God shows off His power again by defying the impossible. His servants remain faithful to worshiping Him and Him alone. As a result, not only does God reveal Himself to them by keeping them safe in the furnace, He also shows His glory to the ones who are witnessing it happen. Nebuchadnezzar is amazed at what he sees and knows exactly who is responsible.

²⁸ Then Nebuchadnezzar said, "Praise be to the God of Shadrach, Meshach and Abednego, who has sent his angel and rescued his servants! They trusted in him and defied the king's command and were willing to give up their lives rather than serve or worship any god except their own God. ²⁹ Therefore I decree that the people of any nation or language who say anything against the God of Shadrach, Meshach and Abednego be cut into pieces and their houses be turned into piles of rubble, for no other god can save in this way."

Daniel 3:28-29 (NIV)

Do you see what happened here? God presented one of His extraordinary events, the king was able to witness the manifested divine intervention, and the king's heart changed completely. It's astounding how your life changes when you finally see God in a real way.

PRESENT DAY EXAMPLES

There are countless times throughout the ages where God has intervened on human affairs.

Jesus comes to Earth (by way of a miracle), and God continues to reveal Himself through extreme acts. One of the biggest parts of Jesus' ministry was healing. Every time He healed someone of their sickness or handicap, He was making Himself more tangible to them and the people around them. Jesus's life was full of miracles including bringing His friend, Lazarus, back to life after he had already died (John 11:1-44). In John 6, the disciples are out in a boat and suddenly find Jesus walking on water (John 6:19). His life was a slideshow of doing things that were not supposed to be done. Nature tells us that once you're dead, you're dead. God had other plans. Next time you go to the beach or the pool, try the whole walking on water trick. Chances are, you won't be able to accomplish what He did. There are some crazy stories in the Bible where some remarkable events took place. I'm telling you, the Bible is an interesting read. God never misses an opportunity to reveal Himself to His people in powerful ways. The unfortunate tragedy, however, is that we have developed a pattern of overlooking His work.

  We seem to think these days that those huge miracles God ordained are simply lost in the past. I've heard many people exclaim how they wish God would perform miracles today like He did in the Bible. HE DOES! We have just failed to notice. Again and again, a miracle is when God makes things happen that go against the rules of nature. There are many examples of God's intervening every time the sun rises, but I don't have time to mention them all. Go talk to any person who works in the medical field and has witnessed cancer disappear like it was never there or has seen something happen when something else was supposed to happen.

    There is one specific miracle I have been blessed to witness multiple times. I could mention every case, but we don't have enough time or pages. I am talking about the miracle of salvation. When we think about the technical definition of what a true miracle is and what God's intentions are in performing these miracles, the moment one of His human creations turns to follow Him is one of the greatest qualifiers. All the examples we looked at contain an event where the laws of nature were overruled. Think about the nature of people. Ever since the fall of man, we have had a sin problem. We are born with a sinful nature. I will re-form that sentence to make more sense. It is in our nature to rebel and go against what is good. Nature says that we are *supposed* to sin. Our human affairs are filled with dirty hearts. When God reveals Himself to one of His children and they actually see Him for the first time, that sinful nature is defied and a miracle is formed. It is an absolute miracle when a teenager, whose parents left them as a child causing them to feel abandoned, unloved, and alone, turns from the pattern of this world to follow Jesus. It is an absolute miracle when the fatherless finally see their Father. It is an absolute miracle when a drug addict finds full satisfaction in the grace of God. Don't tell me miracles are lost in the past. Jesus has not returned yet, which tells us God has some more work He wants to do.

DUE CREDIT

One unfortunate truth is that there are a lot of people out there who are very skeptical when it comes to the idea of a miracle. This world is filled with cause-and-effect relationships. If something happens, there was something else that caused it to happen. Scientists and people who are probably much more intelligent than myself fill their time with assigning credit where credit is due. This is what we do when we research the cause-and-effect relationships. We observe the effect and give credit to whatever caused the effect. I'm beginning to confuse myself, but stay with me. Let me give a couple examples: "We have different seasons because of the earth's tilt. The earth's tilt gets the credit for why we have warmer and cooler seasons." Here's another one: "A baby is conceived when a male and female have intercourse. The male and female get the credit for a baby being born." This is how the world works. Things happen as a result of other things happening beforehand. Scientists are all about assigning credit where credit is due.

Here's where the problem lies. People are always trying to assign credit where credit is due except when it comes to miracles. We have actually gotten to a point where we accept the fact that if we cannot explain it, it must be a miracle. A miracle has become anything that happens without knowledge of who the credit should go to. The truth is that miracles work the same way as everything else in the universe! Miracles happen because God intervened on human affairs and revealed Himself by doing something extraordinary. Is it just me, or is this the same type of cause-and-effect relationship as my previous examples? If science is about having knowledge of which cause gets the credit for each effect, why should huge events be any different than normal events? The same truth applies. God gets the credit for doing something that man cannot do. God gets the credit for creating nature and all of its laws. God gets the credit when events happen that defy and overrule the laws of nature. If our society's goal is to assign credit where credit is due, it's time God get's His share.

THE TRUE MYSTERY

Miracles have become such a mystery to us all. That's part of the reason so many people are intrigued by them. When we claim that something has no cause, and it just happens without any sort of explanation, it becomes an enormous mystery. This is why we are so captivated by secret admirers. We know someone is attracted to us, but we don't know who it is. We receive a fancy letter without the knowledge of where it came from. We don't know the source. We don't know who to give credit to. When the cause of an effect is unknown, there is great mystery involved. The massive misconception, however, is that the miracles themselves are the actual mysteries of the universe.

If miracles are extraordinary events manifesting divine intervention in human affairs, we are given both the cause and the effect. The effects are the extraordinary events, and the cause is the divine intervention. Do I need to go back to my handy dictionary to see what "divine" means?

Divine- Of, relating to, or proceeding directly from God or a god.

I'm not talking about *a* god; I'm talking about *the* God, the God of gods, the King of kings, the Lord of lords. He is the cause of everything. He gets the credit. So, if we are following this scientific truth and if miracles do, in fact, have a direct cause, where is the mystery?

I agree that there is still something enigmatic about miracles. The miracles themselves are not the mystery, but a mystery is still present nonetheless. As a review, we are able to witness two things when observing a miracle: the extraordinary event and the divine intervention. One is the effect, and one is the cause. What if the actual mystery was not the effect, but rather, the cause? If there are only two options, and the extraordinary event is not the mystery, it only leaves the divine intervention. We've already discussed how when a miracle happens, we are being given the gift of tangibly seeing God at work. This is where the mystery lies. It is completely logical to label God as a mystery. I fully believe everything I have read about what God has done, but that does not mean I fully comprehend it. I can't fathom how God can simply speak life into existence, but I believe it. My mind can't grasp the thought of how God can give me His undivided attention while doing the same thing for anyone else at the exact same moment, but I believe it. It is extremely difficult for me to process the thought God having no beginning or end, but I believe it. As humans, we like to fully understand concepts before putting all of our faith and trust into them. The only problem is actually not a problem at all. God is too big for us to understand. If you can fully understand your god, your god is not big enough.

Here is the beautiful thing. God is so big that we cannot begin to understand or comprehend His being. Isaiah testifies to this:

[8] *"For my thoughts are not your thoughts,*
neither are your ways my ways,"
declares the LORD.
[9] *"As the heavens are higher than the earth,*
so are my ways higher than your ways
and my thoughts than your thoughts.

Isaiah 55:8-9 (NIV)

Every time you are able to witness a miracle, God is allowing you to see a glimpse of Him. That is where the mystery comes from. We are seeing something that is much bigger than we can possibly imagine. What is so compelling is that every time we see God through His work in miracles, it is so savory and sweet that nothing else will ever satisfy us the way we are fulfilled when He manifests Himself. It is a beautiful mystery, and we can't get enough. The next time you ask for a miracle, be ready for a divine intervention.

Chapter 8

The Hill in the Race
It may take some suffering to see God.

One of my favorite holidays has always been Independence Day. There are so many things I love about the Fourth of July: the warm weather, the cookouts, the fireworks, and the realization that I have the freedom to worship the God who made me however I want. It all puts me in a great mood. One particular thing I remember about this day of freedom is that my father would always run the great Peachtree Road Race in downtown Atlanta. The 10K race through the heart of the city is a tradition for many avid runners in the metro area. My dad would always join the 60,000 runners with his tank top and bright yellow headband. Sexy right?

He has recently retired from running the race, and this past Fourth of July was my wife's and my valiant debut. I was so excited that I went out and bought one of those Camelbak backpacks that have the water straws leading straight to your mouth. I was so ready and fully expected to be one of the elite runners. I have always been involved in physical activity and consider myself to be rather fit. I had also just finished going through the Insanity workouts to prepare for the race. As soon as Kim and I got to the transit station the morning of the race, we started hearing various people talking about the dreaded cardiac hill. Kim got a little intimidated, but I knew this hill would be no match for me. Can I get an "amen" from the men? The hill was approximately halfway through the race and the crest of the hill was right across from Piedmont Hospital. It was pretty conveniently placed in case the hill got the best of those who dared to try.

    I started out strong running the first few miles, and I was in the zone. I was passing people like crazy and had my rhythmic breathing working for me. I reached the start of cardiac hill with the utmost confidence I could avoid stopping. After a few hundred feet, I had to breathe a little harder but had to continue. About halfway up the hill, I started feeling it. It was like how I feel after my first full plate at Thanksgiving dinner. I kept jogging, but I think the speed-walkers were able to pass me at this point. Finally, I was a few hundred feet away from the top of the hill when my body was shouting, "NO!" I gave it my best, but I had to stop and walk. I hated that the hill caused me to slow down, but the important thing was that my wife and I did, in fact, finish the race. It felt so rewarding knowing we got through it all and reached the coveted finish line. It was definitely not as easy as I thought it would be. Even though I was in shape and considered myself ready to endure, running a long race is very tough. No matter how fit one may be, there will always be something that pushes you to your limits. This is actually the very thing most runners love about running. They love being pushed to their limits and being able to overcome.

Every race has a hill. The hill is the hardest part of the race, it makes running much more difficult, it causes you to slow down, and it makes you feel as though there is no way you can continue. I find it quite interesting how life tends to be the same way. Life is not a sprint; it's a marathon. We've all heard that before. Paul also compares his life to a race in his second letter to Timothy:

⁷ I have fought the good fight, I have finished the race, I have kept the faith.
                                    2 Timothy 4:7 (ESV)

Life is a race that we have all been involuntarily volunteered to run. All of us can testify that there are hills in every race. There are things in life that push us to our limits and make us want to quit, but every runner knows one thing. The reward of finishing makes every hill worth it.

IT'S ALL RELATIVE

I always find it so humorous when people are asked about women's suffrage. I am completely FOR it, but I don't think a lot of people know what it means. It is funny because as soon as you hear their response to what they think about women's suffrage, you also find out if they know what it means. I am not trying to pick on these people because I completely understand why they think women's suffrage constitutes the suffering of women. What a horrible word to describe something good! Suffrage is so close to suffer, when hearing the word, we automatically think it is related to something dreadful. No one thinks women should have to suffer for being women.

This chapter is not about having the right to vote, but it is about the word that encapsulates a negative context. SUFFERING. Most of us just had chills run down our spines. If we were to all give our own definition of what it means to suffer, everyone's definition would probably be unique. A great, simple, and global description I think we can all agree on would more than likely look like this.

Suffer- To go through something that sucks.

Sounds profound, right? That pretty much wraps it up. All of us have been through a time in our life when the only direction left to go is up. Things couldn't get any worse, and we feel absolutely alone in trying to overcome. You are probably thinking of a time at this moment when you went through a time of suffering. You may be going through it right now. One thing I can say with absolute confidence is that we have all been there, and we can all say, there is nothing good about suffering. Everything about the word screams darkness.

Another interesting truth about suffering is that it is one of the most relative things in the world. We all tend to suffer in our own ways, and one way is no worse than another. As humans, we do like to compete with each other with our levels of suffering, but there is really no way to define an absolute when it comes to suffering. It all depends on who you are. It's like the debate of what hurts worse: childbirth or getting kicked in the family jewels? A lot of us, including myself, would promptly argue that childbirth wins by a mile, but when it comes down to it, there really *is* no way of testing that. We all suffer in our own ways. How I suffer is going to be different than the way Kim suffers.

There is another example. When I first started teaching, I went through the roughest week of my life. I became overwhelmed with anxiety and panic. This resulted in losing ten pounds because I had no appetite and couldn't keep anything down, I was constantly tired because I couldn't sleep, and a brown paper bag became my best friend. This was very uncharacteristic for me, but I quickly found out that dealing with anxiety and panic was the fastest way to bring me to my knees. One of my colleagues started teaching the same time I did, but took a very different road of struggle. She became a host for migraine after migraine. In my head, I would much rather deal with a headache than anxiety, but physical pain is what really got to her.

We all suffer from something at some point in our lives. The only difference is the dress suffering wears when it shows its ugly face. For some, it's harder to run uphill. Others struggle more with running downhill. It is all relative. The only absolute we can rely on when it comes to suffering is that it *will* happen no matter who you are. Jesus even warns us it is going to happen. Look at how Jesus alerts us in Scripture:

"...In this world you will have trouble..."
John 16:33b (NIV)

He tells us ahead of time! He does not use any words like if, might, some, or possibly. He proclaims it as a promise. You WILL have trouble. It does not matter who you are, where you live, what you do, or how smart you may be. If you are in this world, you will experience trouble. It may all be relative to who you are, but one unfortunate truth is certain, you *will* go through suffering in this world. No one can avoid the hill in the race.

SETTING THINGS STRAIGHT

This whole topic of suffering is a very sensitive issue, especially when it comes to connecting it with God. We all agree that we have had to suffer with something at some point in our lives. One problem we have, however, is when we think about the source of suffering. Where does it come from? Why does it happen? Why does it happen to *me*? We finally arrive at the bottom of our pit, and immediately we start looking for an explanation. It is unfortunate to be found in our lowest point, but what's more devastating is where we point our finger.

So many of us ask this question: If God loves us so much, why does He make us suffer? If God can do all things and knows all things and is all-powerful and loving, why would a loving God cause us to go through so much pain? We ask this question with our fists clinched and finger pointed towards God as if He owes us an explanation. Then we come to resent this "higher power" and tragically turn from Him while never looking back. If God were real, He would have been there for me. He wouldn't have made me go through such opposition. Some of us have been at this point, and some of us are standing right in the middle of it.

This is one of the most disastrous misconceptions people have concerning the nature of God.

I think it's time we set things straight. God is NOT a bully with a magnifying glass trying to see how much His poor little ants can take. Because of our suffering, we have gotten to a point where we are bitter towards God and can't think of why He would do such a thing. To get past this blurred idea of His character, we must go back and take a look at His intention for creating us in the first place. First of all, no one commands God to do anything. If God created something, it was because He wanted to. Understanding this simple concept should help us to see that God created man and woman because He wanted them to exist, not because He wanted something to torture. Look at Genesis 1:28 for evidence:

> *^{28} And God blessed them. And God said to them, "Be fruitful and multiply and fill the earth and subdue it, and have dominion over the fish of the sea and over the birds of the heavens and over every living thing that moves on the earth."*
>
> Genesis 1:28 (ESV)

We were created in the image of God, and as such, He blessed us and gave us dominion over everything on the earth. We had a relationship with God, and it was good. No suffering. You see, we like to blame God for "making" us suffer, but that was not the intention of this loving God. Every one of God's plans are good. We have already looked at what happens next in the story. Satan comes in, as you can see in Genesis 3, and blurs the vision of God's most famous creations. As we are talking about suffering and what makes us suffer, let's look at what happens right after the two humans sin against the God who made them.

> *And they heard the sound of the LORD God walking in the garden in the cool[l] of the day, and the man and his wife hid themselves from the presence of the LORD God among the trees of the garden.*
>
> Genesis 3:8 (ESV)

As soon as they disobeyed God's words, shame and embarrassment filled their hearts because of the weight of sin. Did you catch what happened? They hid themselves! God did not hide them. They separated themselves from the presence of God. What is more amazing is the fact that God even chose to seek them out after He knew they did not keep up their end of the deal. God *does* give the humans consequences because no sin can go unpunished. If you think that's unfair of God, go ask any parent what they think about giving consequences for disobedience. Some of the consequences of sin include shame, guilt, embarrassment, and physical pains for both the man and woman (childbirth...ouch!). These effects aren't great, but the real consequences came next. Along with the current list, humans now had to deal with death, a required payment for sin, and probably the worst of them all, separation from God. They were kicked out of the garden (Genesis 3:23-24, ESV).

We are still wrestling with the question, "Why do we suffer?" So far, God created man and gave him life, man sinned against God, man hid from God, and man was separated from God. Let's take a look at what happens to anything that is separated from its life source. Picture a goldfish that is taken out of its bowl. It starts flopping around like crazy and gets to a point where it cannot breathe, so it lies there slowly fighting for breath. It is suffering because it was separated from where it was supposed to be. Think of your cell phone. You use it all day by talking, texting, searching the web, playing games, and for some of us, listening to music. What happens to the battery the more you use your phone? Its life continues to descend the more you use it. If you do not connect your phone to a power source, what happens? It dies. It suffers because it is separated from its life source for too long. I can think of a number of examples, but it does not take much for us to understand that if a creation is separated from its life source, the only thing to be expected is a life that ultimately suffers.

When humans sinned against God, they hid themselves and separated themselves from the very thing that gave them life. God is not the one who makes us suffer. WE have to suffer because of what WE did. It's like we are children who have run away from home and have blamed our parents because it's cold.

Our sin is the reason we all go through suffering. Most of the time, bad things happen to us based on two determiners: We made a bad decision, or someone else made a bad decision that directly affected us. I can't help but think of a car accident involving a drunk driver and an innocent driver. There are only two possible outcomes to this unfortunate situation. The drunk driver gets killed, or the innocent person gets killed. Either way, something awful happens based on one bad decision.

When we suffer, we always want to point the finger at God. God is the source of *good* things. With Satan's overwhelming help, *we* are the source of bad things. If something bad happens, if we struggle, if we suffer, we have to take a look at the source. Feeling good yet? My goal is not to make us all depressed with low self-esteem. The objective is simply to set things straight by understanding that God did not create us with the intention of having us suffer. Since we all have sinned, we are all separated from God. Since we are all separated from God, we all go through suffering. We have disconnected ourselves from our life source.

TAKE HEART

I feel like I'm currently on an episode of *Mythbusters*. The myth that God makes us suffer is finally BUSTED! Even though the question, "Why does God **make** us suffer," has proven itself to be inaccurate, our curiosity is completely understandable. We have every right to examine the reasons for our struggles. In fact, it is not only acceptable for us to do so, but it is beneficial as well. To help us out, I am going to make our question much more precise by changing one simple word. Why does God **allow** us to suffer?

This question is much more accurate because we are still getting answers without God's character being compromised. It actually enhances His character by showing His authority over everything. When Job was beginning to suffer in the midst of being a righteous man, it was only because God allowed Satan to inflict it. God *does* allow us to suffer, but there is one thing we now know about our God. Everything He does is for His glory and our good. That being said, He allows us to suffer because He knows good will come of it.

> [20] *You intended to harm me, but God intended it for good to accomplish what is now being done, the saving of many lives.*
> Genesis 50:20 (NIV)

So what kind of good can come from suffering? We naturally think that suffering leads to death, but luckily, our God is the maker of life. If you've read through this entire chapter, you're probably at a point where you want to throw this book down and go hide in a corner. Stay with me because this is finally where the rays of light start to pierce through the tunnel. You don't want to miss what's coming next. Through my own experience suffering and from listening and learning from many others' experiences, I have come up with three reasons God allows us to go through suffering:

1. So we can become stronger and more mature.
2. So He can be the hero.
3. So we can become more like Him.

STRONGER

God allows us to suffer so we can become stronger and more mature. This concept is very difficult for us to see when we are in the middle of it. Whether we see it or not, however, it is an idea that is actually very easy for us to understand. As I have mentioned, physical fitness is a fairly big interest of mine. Ever since middle school, I have been lifting weights or going through some type of conditioning to ensure my body is in tip-top shape. I have been around football for most of my life as a player and a coach, so I can speak on this with a little bit of credibility. Every football player works out for one reason, to get stronger. Athletes are not going to put themselves through all that if there is no benefit for doing so. We push our bodies to the limits to get stronger and to expand our limits. We look forward to running uphill to increase our tolerance of each hill.

Let's say you are someone who has never picked up a weight or has never worked out in your life. You finally reach a point where you want to become stronger, so you join a gym and begin working out. You feel awesome that first day and walk out like you've conquered the world. Then comes the next two or three days and reality hits you. You can't go to the bathroom without your entire body flooding with pain. You become so sore, it's hard to even walk or laugh. You have a choice at this time in your life. You can let the pain get the best of you and throw in the towel, or you can work though the pain and reach a new level of physical maturity. Those are your only two options. When we work out, we push our muscles to their limits, and what we are actually doing is destroying and tearing our muscle fibers. (My physical education history is coming out a bit). In a nutshell, this tearing causes inflammation of our muscles, which makes them really sore. The good news, however, is that when the muscle finally recovers, the fibers return more numerous than before. This is what actually makes your muscle, as a whole, stronger. There is a catch though. In order for you to become stronger and for your body to overcome the soreness and pain, you have to stay with it. If you throw in the towel, every time you try to start up again, you can expect the same fate.

I know this has been a lengthy illustration, but I hope you are getting the idea. In many areas of our life, we understand that things tend to get a little worse before they get better. To become stronger and more physically mature, there is no way to avoid the soreness and pain that come with it. Like I said, when flooded with pain, we are at a fork in the road. We can quit, or we can push through and reach a new height.

What God is actually doing when He allows us to suffer is providing us with an opportunity. He is giving us the chance to become sore so that we can eventually become stronger and more mature. James, the brother of Jesus, actually mentions this directly in the Bible:

> *²Consider it pure joy, my brothers and sisters, whenever you face trials of many kinds, ³because you know that the testing of your faith produces perseverance. ⁴Let perseverance finish its work so that you may be mature and complete, not lacking anything.*
>
> James 1:2-4 (NIV)

We always think God is taking away from us when we go through suffering, but what He is really doing is equipping us. He does not want you to lack anything. He wants you to become stronger, and sometimes, it takes a little bit of soreness and pain to get there.

MY HERO

God allows us to suffer so He can be the hero. We have to be careful with this one because we can so easily twist the meaning. This is not saying God is like a politician who raises taxes and lowers them later to make himself look better. That is not the direction we are heading. Again, God allows us to suffer because He knows something good for us and for Him can come of it.

In the time that I have been with Kim, there have been a few times when she was in trouble. There is one specific time that comes to mind. We were spending the weekend at one of our mutual friend's lake house, and we all decided to go tubing in the lake. For this group, tubing got a little nasty. They did everything they could while driving the boat to create the biggest wipeout possible. It was exciting, entertaining, and pretty hilarious. It was time for Kim and I to brave the dangerous, tubing waters. We both started out great, which gave the boat drivers even more motivation to flip our tubes. Sure enough, Kim and I eventually hit this huge wave that sent us flying into the air and each other. As soon as I hit the water, all I could think about was if she was okay. I came up to the surface only to find her in great pain. My heart instantly sank, and all of my concern and attention went to helping her get through it. The only thing I could really do, though, was wrap my arms around her and tell her that everything was going to be fine. Kim and I had only been dating for a few months at this point, but this incident revealed to me how much I actually cared about her.

Kim and I would both agree that, although it seemed scary at the time, that circumstance brought us to a new point in our relationship. I hated seeing Kim in pain, but I loved getting the opportunity to be her hero. Being married, we run into unfortunate events all the time, and the same truth applies. There are days when she is exhausted from work, there are times when someone hurts her feelings, and there are times when she gets hurt physically. I hate to see her in any type of pain, but I relish the opportunities to restore her strength. It's as if every struggle we share brings us closer together.

Any parent feels the same way about their children. You hate to see your child suffer, but you love it when they come to you for help. You have the opportunity to restore them, to save them, and to be their hero! Every tragic event has a supernatural way of bringing you closer together. It is no different with God. Can you imagine how God feels for us?

We always love the hero in the story! Why? Because the hero is the one that helps us overcome, the one who defeats the enemy, and the one who gets things back to the way they are supposed to be. We go through a lot of suffering in our lives, and God allows it because He sees these situations as something different. He sees these events as opportunities to come through for us and to bring us to a new level in our relationship with Him. He is a good God and loves when we see Him as such. The fact that God wants to be the hero shows us that we have nothing to fear when it comes to suffering. I mentioned a portion of John 16:33 a little earlier, but let's look at what Jesus says next.

> *³³ "I have told you these things, so that in me you may have peace. In this world you will have trouble. But take heart! I have overcome the world."*

John 16:33 (NIV)

He guarantees trouble in this world, but He finishes with an incredible promise. Take heart! I have overcome everything you could possibly face in this world. Every little thing that we could imagine and every circumstance we could go through is covered by God's promise to be our hero. There is an enemy that is going to do everything he can to make you quit, but there is good news. Everything Satan uses to destroy you, God uses to bring you back to life. I can just see Satan getting pissed off every time that happens, and I love it! He has the perfect plan to finally bring you to your knees, and God takes advantage by using that very plan to bring you even closer to Himself. Suffering gives us the perfect opportunity to run to God and gives Him the perfect opportunity to, once again, be our hero.

HE GETS IT

God allows us to suffer so we can become more like Him. This is probably the most important and greatest benefit we can acquire as a result of our suffering. I confidently make that statement because the more you are able to relate to something, the more real it becomes in your life. The more real something becomes in your life, the more you tend to notice it on a daily basis. Since our ongoing goal in this book is to see God in a more tangible and existent way, I would say relating to Him is of the utmost importance.

As humans, we tend to find great comfort when we can relate to one another. We are always looking for things we have in common with someone else. People always claim that opposites attract, but on the larger level of things, I would have to disagree. We like to have things in common because, as a result, we are able to understand each other better. Generally, the more we are able to understand each other, the more of a connection we are able to make. There is a saying that has always stood out to me: A good friend will bail you out of jail, but a *best* friend will be in jail right beside you. I disagree with this statement, but I get the logic.

Why isn't the friend who bailed you out of jail the best friend? In reality, they actually did more good for you than the other friend. The other friend probably even caused your life more trouble. It sounds completely logical, but for some reason, we don't seem to see it that way. I think it all comes to the shared experience. You and the friend in jail with you have something in common that the good friend will never have. The two of you shared something together, you went through something together, and you now have a story to tell…together. It actually has nothing to do with what your friends do *for* you. It has everything to do with what your friends do *with* you. The biggest thing that makes the distinction between a good friend and a best friend is what you are able to share. In fact, even the bad things that happen to us essentially don't seem quite as bad when we have company. Again, misery loves company. This is because, as humans, we are built to relate to each other. We don't like feeling alone in our circumstance. That is what makes suffering so unbearable in the first place

It is truly amazing how a connection with someone else can change your outlook on the situation. The reason we become so bitter towards God is because we lack that connection when it comes to suffering. We are deceived into thinking that God has never had to go through what we are going through. We look at God as the suspect to our suffering rather than a fellow victim. When God came to Earth as the person of Jesus, He did something unimaginable. Most of us know what happened to Jesus when He was here. If you have never heard the story, there is a brief synopsis in the second chapter of Paul's letter to the Philippians.

> *[6] "who, though he was in the form of God, did not count equality with God a thing to be grasped, [7] but emptied himself, by taking the form of a servant, being born in the likeness of men. [8] And being found in human form, he humbled himself by becoming obedient to the point of death, even death on a cross.*
> Philippians 2:6-8 (ESV)

We always look at God as something that we cannot understand and something we have no chance in connecting with. Yes, it is impossible to fully comprehend the nature of God, but look at what He did so we could connect with Him better. God left all His glory and took the form of a servant. He made Himself nothing! He turned Himself into a human knowing full well what we were going to do to Him. The King lowered Himself and took the role of a king's servant. Why would He do that? The eighth verse shows a little picture of the suffering Jesus went through. His own people spit in His face, mocked Him, beat Him, tortured Him, humiliated Him, and killed Him. They made Him suffer, and He took it all willingly. It doesn't make sense does it?

Jesus took on all of the suffering because, as God, He knew something we did not. He knew the only way we would ever be able to fully relate with Him is putting Himself in our situation. When Jesus was on the cross, He took on the full wrath of God, which caused Him to be completely separated from God. We already talked about how, because of our sin, we are also separated from God. Going through everything Jesus went through gave Him complete authority to be able to say, "I've been there!" Isn't it amazing how those words seem to get rid of the loneliness? I get it. I'm with you. I understand. Been there, done that. We have something in common! Look at how Jesus encourages us in John 15:

> *"If the world hates you, keep in mind that it hated me first."*
> John 15:18 (NIV)

I love this statement by Jesus! He is reassuring us that everything we face here on Earth, He has already faced. You're lonely? Jesus was too. You're mocked? Jesus was too. You're physically assaulted? Jesus was too. You are neglected? Jesus was too. You are hated? Jesus was too. He went through everything we could imagine. He knows how you feel, and He has felt your pain. What Jesus miraculously did when He came to Earth was take on both of the "friend" identities. He did something unbelievable *for* us, but He was also going through something *with* us. When you are running up your steepest hill and life is pushing you more than you can bear, try imagining yourself right across from Jesus as He's getting beaten. Picture yourself staring at Him straight in His blood-filled eyes with

Him glaring back at you. You can almost hear Him say, "Let's do this! I'm right here with you." Seeing yourself in the same scene as Jesus can do wonders in helping you relate to God better.

If we feel closer to people we experience things with, there is nothing that can keep us from relating to God. Maybe God is allowing you to suffer because He wants to draw you closer to Himself. Maybe He wants you to see that He is a God who understands your situation and wants nothing more than for you to see the reality of who He is. Maybe God is allowing you to be brought to your knees because He knows that's the place you can most clearly see Him.

A FINAL THOUGHT

Jesus tells us to take heart. He tells us to keep pressing on. He encourages us in this way because He has already experienced the joy that comes when you have endured through the struggle. The joy is why He chose to endure in the first place.

> *"For the joy set before him he endured the cross, scorning its shame, and sat down at the right hand of the throne of God."*
> Hebrews 12:2 (NIV)

What Jesus is doing here is showing us that we can have hope in the midst of our suffering. We look at our difficult circumstance with a scold, but what we have actually found is that the benefits far outweigh the costs. When we suffer, we have the opportunity to become stronger and more mature, to be rescued by the Hero of heroes, and we have the opportunity to relate to God and see Him in a way we never have before. There is impeccable joy waiting on the other side of suffering. Jesus has run the race, marked the trail, and has already reached the top of the hill. He is calling out begging for us to keep running and keep fighting because it is worth it!

I love the picture of a group of people running a marathon together. I especially enjoy the end of the race. What you commonly find is a straggler who got left in the crowd and is bringing up the rear. The runner thinks everyone has left, and he's running this race on his own. Then, all of a sudden, you see runners who have already finished running back towards him to cheer him on. They start running beside him just as his motivation reaches an unprecedented level. He finally finishes with a burst of energy and is overwhelmed with joy as his peers applaud his perseverance.

Every time we go through a time of suffering, Jesus is running towards us from the finish line to cheer us on and finish the race with us. We think we are running alone, but He has never left. He is screaming, "You can do it! I'm with you!" We can all connect with God better through our suffering. Seeing God's ability to go through what we go through has an incredible way of making His presence more real. My challenge to you is to change your perspective. Instead of viewing your moment of suffering as punishment from God, try looking at it as an opportunity He is giving you to relate to Him better. When you get to the top of the hill and look back, you might be surprised at how willing you are to keep going.

Chapter 9

The Simple Equation
It may take love to see God.

We are all gifted in different areas when it comes to education. As for me, I was always a math guy. Believe it or not, literature and English were always my worst subjects. I was really good with numbers, and my mind was able to put things together fairly quickly. That being said, people hated me and loved me in math class when I was in high school and college. They hated me because most of the equations just clicked for me without much trouble, and they did not have the same ability. They loved me, however, because they knew that they needed my help. A new equation would be introduced, I would put it all together and be able to finish my work, and then I would spend the rest of the time helping my peers to see the equation as I saw it. I am not trying to make myself sound like a genius because I am far from it, but I had one goal. Keep it simple. While trying to aid my peers, I noticed a common aspect to their approach. Most of them were taking a simple equation and making it more complicated. Some of the time, they would feel silly when they finally realized the solution because the answer was right in front of them the whole time. They just didn't see it.

I have noticed that this problem is not only found in the classroom, but is present in other aspects of life as well. Specifically, we see it a lot when it comes to relationships and the topic of love. Some of us have seen those people (or happen to be those people) who always seem to find relationships complicated. Don't you love it when you find a friend on Facebook, and their relationship status reads, "It's complicated?" It's like they are in a relationship, kind of, but not really. It is… complicated. They are trying to deal with the issue and figure the whole thing out while most of us have already figured it out and know exactly what is going to happen. To us, looking in, it's really not that complex. It's pretty simple. I think the majority of us have been on both sides of this situation. We have been in the relationship, and we have observed others' relationships. Since most of us have experience in this area, I think we can be real with one another. Don't we have a way of making things more complicated than they need to be?

We are doing this more and more when it comes to the topic of love. Some of us spend most of our lives trying to *find* love while the rest of us are trying to figure out *how* to love. Love has become so complicated and such a mystery to the universe. We are doing everything we can to figure out the solution, but we keep reaching a dead end. What if it didn't have to be so hard? What if the answer was right in front of us the whole time? We are making a simple equation more complicated than it has to be.

All you math-haters stay with me. Look at this equation: $A=B$. You can read it again if you need to. I think we can all agree that this is a simple equation. If $A=B$, when you have B, you must also have A. They are dependent upon each other, which means you cannot have one without the other. If you have A, you have B. If you show A, you show B. This is the simple concept that we have blown out of proportion. It is not difficult, but we seem to see it that way. This equation is going to be our foundation throughout this chapter, so it is critical that we understand it. If $A=B$, then $B=A$. If this equation is easy to understand, the rest of the chapter will fall into place. Topics like God and love are seen as extremely deep and difficult to define, but to avoid the complications, there is only one thing we can do. Keep it simple.

WHAT IS LOVE?

It's hard for me to hear "what is love" without also hearing "baby don't hurt me..." *Night at the Roxbury* anybody? On a more serious note, think if someone came up to you and asked you that question. What is love? (It just happened again) I think we would all probably have a different answer. We have turned love into this relative concept, and we allow it to mean whatever people want it to mean. This is where things get complicated. Remember, our goal is to keep it simple. I am not going to offend anyone by expressing what love is not because, frankly, that's not my place and the Bible can take care of that for me. Instead, I want us to look at a very clear, simple, and straight up answer for what love is. It doesn't take much to understand it. Ask Forrest Gump. My references are on fire right now!

We are going to look at a clear definition of love because I believe that was God's intention. If this is the greatest thing He called us to do, I think

He would make it clear and straight to the point. The definition is found in one of the most famous chapters of the Bible. It is actually well known as the love chapter. You may not be a Christian, but chances are, you have heard this passage at least once in your life. If you have ever been to a wedding, you have probably witnessed this passage being read or referenced. It is found in chapter thirteen of Paul's first letter to the Corinthians.

> *"⁴ Love is patient, love is kind. It does not envy, it does not boast, it is not proud. ⁵ It does not dishonor others, it is not self-seeking, it is not easily angered, it keeps no record of wrongs. ⁶ Love does not delight in evil but rejoices with the truth. ⁷ It always protects, always trusts, always hopes, always perseveres. ⁸ Love never fails..."*

1 Corinthians 13:4-8 (NIV)

What is love? It is patient. It is kind. It is satisfied. Paul actually gives us a definition stating exactly what love is. It is not something that needs to be figured out or solved. It is kept simple. This is what love is. He does not express love as a feeling or something that is hard to describe. He gives a straight answer to make his point as clear as possible. The problem is that we have blurred the transparency of love. Some people would say love is a feeling. Some would say it is a specific relationship. The problem with that way of thinking is that defining love in that way makes it tragically temporary. You hear about so many couples breaking up or getting divorced because they "fell out of love." Love is not something you can fall into or out of. Love is something you show. A verb is any word that reflects action. A noun is something that can be manipulated. A feeling is a noun. It can rise and fall and can be lost and found. A feeling is temporary. A feeling can be complicated. Love, however, is a verb. You can show patience, and it has a permanent effect. Showing patience is hard to do but simple to understand. Can you see the difference? This is a juicy one. A feeling is something we seek for ourselves. Patience, kindness, etc. is something we seek to show for the sake of someone else. One is completely selfish while the other is utterly selfless. Chances are, if you are being selfless, you are showing love without even noticing. This is what love is.

Paul provides us with a simple definition and is basically defining our variables. A=B.

Love=Patience. Love=Kindness. Love=Selfless. If you have patience, you have love. If you show kindness, you show love. If you are being selfless, you are being loving. It is not as complicated as we make it. There is a huge difference between something being hard to understand and something being hard to do. Climbing Mount Everest is not very hard to understand. Climbing the tallest peak in the world means getting to the top. If you keep going up, you're doing it. It is rather simple to grasp the concept. Now, that does NOT make it easy to do. It is one of the toughest tasks to attempt in the world. Ironically, it is also one of the most rewarding when accomplished.

Love does not have to be complicated. Yes, it is one of the most difficult things to do at times, but it is not complicated. It is a simple equation. Love only becomes difficult to understand when we distort its meaning. Keep it simple! The easier something is to comprehend, the more likely we are to attempt it.

MAKING IT SIMPLE

The driving force behind this book is answering the following question: How can God become more tangible or visible in our lives? In other words, how can we see God in a more real way? One of the crazy things about God is that, while He is the biggest, wisest, and most complex being in the world, He chooses to reveal Himself sometimes in the smallest, simplest, and most personal ways. Why would something so big make itself so small? He does it for one reason, for you and me. We have this misconception that God is too out-of-reach for us to see Him in our every day lives. Again, what if it wasn't what we thought? What if God could be more visible and noticeable in your life, and it was simply up to you how often that happened? This section is about turning that wish into a reality.

    This whole chapter has been about defining love and seeing love for what it really is as indicated by the Bible. We found a very clear definition where it was explained that love is actually seen in a number of different ways. When we see those certain things displayed, we are actually seeing love in action. Now that we have a pretty good understanding of that concept, let's throw another wrench into the equation. At first, we found it extremely difficult to determine what love was. Try thinking about another question: What is God? Have you ever truly taken the time to sit and think about how to describe something that is utterly indescribable? Again, people probably have millions of different answers to that question. What is God? Most of our answers will vary depending on our faith, culture, location, financial status, current circumstances, etc.

Each of our descriptions of what or who God is could be very accurate, but this is also what makes God so unfathomable because there are so many different ways to look at Him. Our goal, however, is to try and see Him in a more fathomable way. Wouldn't it be awesome and so much easier if the Bible just gave us a clear definition of what God was just like it did for love? I have good news for you! It does. John, like Paul, provides us with a very clear and simple definition. He actually gives us one of the most powerful pieces of scripture. This passage is so incredible because these few sentences accomplish the goal of revealing God's ultimate desire to reveal Himself. With his well-written description, John explains how God can actually be noticed and visibly seen on a daily basis. Check out what he wrote in his first letter to the church.

⁷ "Dear friends, let us love one another, for love comes from God. Everyone who loves has been born of God and knows God. ⁸ Whoever does not love does not know God, because <u>God is love</u>. ⁹ This is how God showed his love among us: He sent his one and only Son into the world that we might live through him. ¹⁰ This is love: not that we loved God, but that he loved us and sent his Son as an atoning sacrifice for our sins.¹¹ Dear friends, since God so loved us, we also ought to love one another. ¹² No one has ever seen God; but if we love one another, God lives in us and his love is made complete in us."

1 John 4:7-12 (NIV)

Did you catch my little hint? After thousands of pages of history, prophecy, wisdom, and guidance, God is made as clear as possible. God is love. God = Love. Everything that love is, God is as well. When you put the passage in 1 John with the passage in 1 Corinthians, it starts making sense. God is love. Love is patient. God is patient. God is love. Love is kind. God is kind. Do you see what is happening here? I'm going to take what we learned earlier and apply it to this concept. If you show someone kindness, you are showing them love. Now pay attention because this next sentence is so important I am giving you a warning. If God *is* love, when you are showing someone kindness, you are actually showing them God! Most of us had no idea we had the ability to do that.

Love is a big deal when it comes to God. He actually shows us how He feels about it in a story in the book of Matthew. An expert in the law comes and asks Jesus which commandment is greatest, and Jesus' response reveals His desire to reveal Himself. This is huge, so get ready! Jesus replies by saying the greatest commandment is to love God with everything you have, but He adds on to His answer. He goes on to say that there is a second commandment that is just as important. Love your neighbor as yourself (Matthew 22:36-39, NIV). The greatest and most important commandments in the entire Bible have to deal with showing love towards someone. Maybe these two are so important because God knows something we don't. Most of us think when we are showing our neighbor love we are simply following a command. What is actually happening is that we are showing our neighbor God because God *is* love.

God being defined as love is so critical because when we show love towards someone, we are making God more tangible for us *and* for them. It is a rather simple equation when you think about it. When you show love, you show God because God is love. John reveals this truth in the passage we just looked at. Take another glance over the twelfth verse:

> *[12] No one has ever seen God; but if we love one another, God lives in us and his love is made complete in us.*
> 1 John 4:12 (NIV)

The first sentence explains our predicament. No one has ever seen God. God cannot be seen, heard, or touched. God cannot be tangible. This shows why it is so hard for some of us to put our complete faith in God. The only problem is that this argument is beautifully interrupted by a massive and significant BUT! With that one word, John is exclaiming that there is another way! There is hope. If we love one another, God lives in us... If love is in you, God is in you. When love pours out of you, God pours out of you. Every time you are kind, patient, and selfless towards others, God is being made visible. What an incredible gift we have in the ability to love the people around us!

When we truly love our neighbor, we are not merely following a rule or doing God a favor out of obligation. This view makes the act of loving others look more like a chore. When we love, not only are we being obedient to God's greatest two commandments, we are, more importantly, making the presence and tangibility of God a reality. When we love, we are revealing God's ultimate desire to reveal Himself. It is critical that we take advantage of this opportunity.

LOVE IN ACTION

At this point, you may be on board and getting excited to have the opportunity to show love to your neighbor, but then, you hit your first speed bump. "Okay, I know it is important to show love, and I'm ready, but where do I start?" This is a very good question and a question that we have all thought at some point in our lives. What does this love look like? It is important for us to notice something here. It is impossible to show something if you, yourself, have not been shown the very thing you are trying to show. In other words, you cannot give something you do not have. If you have never seen the true love of Christ, there is no way you can fully show it to someone else. That is step one. Maybe you are there, though. Maybe, throughout this book or through some other circumstance, you have seen the true love of God. What's next? For most of us, it's easy to see God's love for us because of the sight of His son on the cross. We get that part. He took the bullet for us, and we are forever grateful. How do we show that same love? Are we supposed to build little crosses every time we have a son? If only there was a clear picture for how we should love our neighbor.

      The good news is that you are not alone in your wonder. We have all thought about what it means to truly love our neighbor. Luckily, there was an expert in the law who was wondering the very same thing we question today. This gentleman asked Jesus how to get eternal life and answered his own question as guided by the Teacher. Then, he went a bit further with his curiosity and tried to trap Jesus. After receiving the wise answer from Jesus about loving God and those around us, the man asked, "Who is my neighbor?" Basically, he was asking the same question we are asking ourselves today. Who is my neighbor? Who do I show love to? What will this kind of love look like? Jesus answers his question and ours by telling a short story in the tenth chapter of Luke.

> *³⁰ In reply Jesus said: "A man was going down from Jerusalem to Jericho, when he was attacked by robbers. They stripped him of his clothes, beat him and went away, leaving him half dead. ³¹ A priest happened to be going down the same road, and when he saw the man, he passed by on the other side. ³² So too, a Levite, when he came to the place and saw him, passed by on the other side. ³³ But a Samaritan, as he traveled, came where the man was; and when he saw him, he took pity on him. ³⁴ He went to him and bandaged his wounds, pouring on oil and wine. Then he put the man on his own donkey, brought him to an inn and took care of him. ³⁵ The next day he took out two denarii and gave them to the innkeeper. 'Look after him,' he said, 'and when I return, I will reimburse you for any extra expense you may have.'*

³⁶ "Which of these three do you think was a neighbor to the man who fell into the hands of robbers?"

³⁷ The expert in the law replied, "The one who had mercy on him."

Jesus told him, "Go and do likewise."
Luke 10:30-37 (NIV)

I love this because Jesus shows us a template, and simply says to go and copy this example. Again, He keeps it simple. Let's look at this story. It is already intriguing to see that the Samaritan was the one to stop and help the man. For most of us, his first extension would have been enough. He helped him by bandaging his wounds. Then, he took the man to a hotel. Bravo! He fixed his wounds *and* gave him a ride. He goes on. He didn't just drop him off. He stayed and took care of him. It says that the Samaritan was traveling on the road, so he was probably going somewhere or had some place to be. Someone may have been expecting him. I don't want to add to Jesus' words, but this simply shows that the Samaritan had to put his schedule and his life temporarily on hold for this man. At this point, we're usually feeling pretty good about ourselves. The Samaritan goes further. Not only does he spend the night taking care of this guy. He then uses his own money to make sure the hospitality continues. Alright, that's enough, we get it! He goes further. He does not just leave and hope for the best. When he's coming back through town, he stops back by the hotel and gives more of his own money for any reimbursements that were needed. Oh and don't forget, he didn't even know the guy! This is the template Jesus gave us.

He gave us a perfect illustration of how we are to love our neighbor and reveal who He is. What we have done, however, is turned it into a convenient kind of love, which looks nothing like His illustration at all. We think showing someone love is merely declaring we will pray for them. This is good to do, but it looks a heck of a lot like the priest in Jesus' story. We will talk more about this in the next chapter, but as we saw with the Samaritan, showing true love costs you something. It cost the Samaritan his time, his donkey, his money, and more of his time. I also don't remember the Samaritan complaining about it or looking for an "I owe you."

God showed His love for us by giving up His only son. It cost Him something. The Samaritan showed that same love by losing himself for the sake of another. Jesus is telling us to go and show that same kind of love, a love that costs you something. This is what it looks like to love your neighbor. This is what it looks like to make God more tangible for someone else. The man who was robbed was shown patience, kindness, mercy, and grace. He was shown love. He was shown God.

FORSHADOWING

What does this kind of love look like in today's world? Jesus, I need a simple answer, not a story, for how I am supposed to love the people around me. Are there better ways to show love than others? The Bible contains so many authors who have written about love, but Jesus makes a bold proclamation as recorded by John. He makes His command extremely clear about what it means to show this kind of love.

> [12] *"This is my commandment, that you love one another as I have loved you.* [13] *Greater love has no one than this, that someone lay*

down his life for his friends.
John 15:12-13 (ESV)

Here is the absolute greatest way to show love to someone else. Lay down your life for them. Does this mean physically laying down your life for someone else like jumping in front of a bullet or a train or something? Maybe. Maybe it's as simple as putting the lives of others before your own. Maybe it's as simple as turning your spare room into a room with a bed for anyone who may need it. Maybe it looks like going completely out of the way and costing you a full tank of gas to take someone where they need to be. It could take the form of a number of different actions.

He told us to love as He loved. What did He do? He took our place on the cross and put our lives above His own. How did God reveal His love for us and ultimately reveal Himself to us? He came to Earth and made a beautiful exchange of a sacrifice. This is one of the most powerful, difficult, yet easiest ways to show the tangibility of God. It is not complicated. It is very simple. When we show kindness, we show love. When we show love, we show God. He loved us and showed Himself to us by making a sacrifice. How can we show others what we have been shown? We can start by following Jesus' example. "Go and do likewise."

Chapter 10

Lose Yourself
It may take a sacrifice to see God.

When you hear the word, sacrifice, various ideas may come to mind. One example may be the idea of a sacrifice in the game of baseball. There are many times throughout a season when a team will make a sacrifice to give their team a better chance at scoring more runs. There is the sacrifice fly ball when one player will hit the ball to the outfield. That player usually gets out and lays down his chance to reach home plate. The silver lining, however, is that even though he may be out, he gives his teammate on third base the chance the score a run for his team. There is another situation where a player will attempt a bunt to advance his teammate to a further base. The hitter usually gets out, but he allows his teammate to move further into scoring position. Every time this happens successfully, you will see the hitter who got out go back to the dugout to be welcomed by a bunch a high fives from his teammates. Why would they congratulate a player who got out? They do it because that player put the team before himself. He laid down his opportunity to increase his average or on-base percentage in order to help the team win. He sacrificed himself to put his team first.

Something else comes to mind when I think of making a sacrifice. Kim and I are still newlyweds, so needless to say, we are still working on building a financial foundation. This requires us to make a lot of sacrifices. We have to sacrifice nicer things we want now so we can have the nicer things later. Not that life is about having the nicest things, but you know what I mean. Being wise with your money is about making sacrifices. We are learning that concept now more than ever.

Perhaps you're not into baseball, and you have never been married. Maybe when *you* think about making a sacrifice, the only thing that comes to mind is the Old Testament with all of their rituals. In the Old Testament, God's people dealt with their sin in a different way than we do today. To pay or make up for their sin, they would sacrifice various animals to God. It may sound weird to us, but this is how it was done. Fill up your sin bucket during the week, get the fattened calf or goat, and sacrifice it at the end of the week as payment. What ever comes to mind when you think of sacrifice, in every example I mentioned, it was about giving something up. Making a sacrifice costs you something.

The aspect of a sacrifice I want to focus in on throughout the entirety of this chapter is picking up where we left off in chapter 9. We saw in John 15 where Jesus explained that the greatest way to show love is to lay down your life for your friends. We already talked about what that may look like, but I want us to realize that the greatest way to show love is through making a sacrifice. It is about the act of giving up yourself for the sake of someone else. There is no better way to show the love of God.

MAMA KNOWS BEST

The fact that *I* am writing this this chapter may make you think I am incredibly effective in laying down my life for others, but this is not the case. This is actually something I struggle with. If we are going by that logic, my mother has every right to write a book on what it means to sacrifice yourself for the sake of another. No one has shown me what it means to put others first more than her. As children, we don't always notice the sacrifice our parents make so we can get to where we need to be in life. We are totally oblivious. It wasn't until a few years ago that I looked back and truly noticed everything my mother had to give up to make sure her children had what they needed. I know I am biased towards *my* mother, but parents all over the world probably have a great understanding of what it means to lay down your life for someone else. Since I can really only speak for *my* mother, that is what I am going to do.

In my physical education studies in college, I learned that there are various ways to teach a lesson. Two methods that are commonly used are teaching by instructing and teaching by demonstrating. Both are effective; it just depends on your audience and what method works best for you. I am the man I am today because of my mother's teachings. She spent so much of her time teaching us through instruction. Every time an opportunity presented itself, she took advantage to help us grow and mature. With every passing circumstance that would arise, mom could turn it into a lesson to be learned. She would instruct us on how to treat others, how to cook, how to bag groceries properly, how to separate clothes when doing laundry, how to think before you speak, how to seek and chase what you want, how to ask the right questions, how to communicate, etc. I could go on forever. She was very good at the instructing part of teaching us how to become mature adults. This was extremely conscious as she did it with purpose, and she was good at it.

What my mother did not realize, however, was how much she was actually teaching us through the method of demonstrating. Unconsciously, my mom was teaching us one of the most valuable lessons in life. Throughout my life, there have been an infinite amount of occasions where my mother has put me ahead of herself. This came very naturally to her, but though she was simply doing what came natural, she was teaching my siblings and me how to put others first.

I was child number three for my mom, so she had already began her journey of making sacrifice after sacrifice. Like I mentioned in the last chapter, laying down your life for someone else is not always as extreme as jumping in front of a bullet for someone. The same message can be communicated with the small things. Here are just a few examples:

- When going out to eat, instead of an elegant Italian cuisine, she chose McDonald's and Captain D's for us.
- When going to the movies, instead of a romantic drama, she chose Space Jam for us.
- When going on vacation, instead of a romantic getaway for two, she chose a crowded beach for us.
- When it comes to saving money, instead of building up her retirement fund, she chose to give all she had to us.
- When the weekends came, instead of building up her dream house, she chose little league and ballet for us.

Again, this is just a sliver of the whole pie. Many parents may say, "Well, that is a parent's job." My mother made it a career, and she was a professional. Every time there was a choice between what she preferred for herself and what we were wanting, she always chose us over herself. My siblings and I are mostly grown up now with only my little sister left as a senior in high school. We are all starting our lives with our own jobs and our new families, but my mom is doing the same thing.

She has spent the last 30 years completely giving herself up for her children. It is finally reaching that time where she has every right to do what *she* wants to do. The only thing is that she probably still won't choose herself over someone else. That is just the heart of my mother. She is constantly laying down her life for her friends whether it is her children or a complete stranger. My mom definitely knows what it means to sacrifice, and she should be the one writing this chapter.

THE ULTIMATE SACRIFICE

We are going to get up to our necks with Jesus in a couple chapters, but it is impossible to discuss the idea of making a sacrifice without mentioning the biggest one in the history of the world. The act of Jesus going to the cross and dying, laying down His life for His friends, is the single most heroic and loving event…ever. This sacrifice is the game-changer. It is what separates Christianity from every other faith in the world. It is the foundation of our faith. There are a few reasons this feat proves to be life-altering:

- **He was the propitiatory sacrifice.**

- **He was the permanent sacrifice.**
- **He was the perfect sacrifice.**

In the book of Leviticus, Moses explains something very intriguing. The Israelites at that time, like the rest of us today, had a sin problem. They were so wishy-washy with their faith in God. They would bow down and worship Him, and the next minute they were building something out of rocks to worship. Rocks. God is one who does not necessarily take sin lightly. As we can grasp from the story of Adam and Eve at creation, God does not let sin go without consequence. The Israelites had a problem with rebelling against God, so He created a way for them to "pay" for their sin. Moses was the middleman between God and His people, and he told the people exactly what God commanded in order for their sins to be forgiven. Leviticus 16 shows the complete description, in detail, of everything they had to do to pay or atone for their sin. So much is involved! When you think about all the little things they had to do in the specific order God commanded, it becomes tiring even reading about it. In a nutshell, they had to make specific sacrifices to pay for their sin. Here is the most important part, though. It's so important that I'm giving a warning prior to revealing the passage. Look what it says:

³⁴ "This is to be a lasting ordinance for you: Atonement is to be made once a year for all the sins of the Israelites."
Leviticus 16:34 (NIV)

God told them that it was a *lasting* ordinance. They had to repeat this tidies process and atone or pay for their sins once a year!
Excuse me while I insult your intelligence, but lasting means that it keeps going on and on. Each singular payment was, therefore, temporary. Each payment was enough…until the next one was needed. I get the same feeling paying rent for my apartment. It satisfies the lender for a month, but next month, another payment will be needed. It is a lasting ordinance, and there is no hope of progress. The Israelites are always going to sin, so there is always going to be a payment required. Then comes Jesus.

We also have a sin problem. Now, I don't see too many people sacrificing goats and bulls to

God these days, but that's just me. In reality, *we* are the ones who deserve death because of our sin.

> *"For the wages of sin is death, but the gift of God is eternal life, through Christ Jesus."*
> Romans 6:23 (NIV)

A wage is something you earn. The wage of sin is death. As a result, if you have sinned, you earn death. Because of our sin, we had something horrific in our future. Our sin was so great, the only thing that could pay for it was the wrath of God being satisfied. That doesn't sound comforting does it? I heard a pastor once describe the wrath of God this way. It is as if we were standing in front of a dam ten million miles wide and ten million miles high filled to the brim with water. Imagine that dam beginning to compromise. Oh the fear that would run through our bones. In an instance, the dam crumbles, and the water comes raging directly towards you. This is what we deserve.

When Jesus died on the cross, when He laid down His life for us, He took our place in front of God's wrath. Going back to this pastor's analogy, imagine all that water rushing towards you. Your eyes are closed, fists are clinched, and your life is flashing before your eyes. Suddenly, a hole one foot in front of you opens up and swallows up every drop of water as you are left standing there. Can you imagine the relief? THAT is what Jesus did when He died on the cross. He took on the wrath of God and made the **propitiatory** sacrifice on our behalf.

There is a huge difference between the sacrifice of the animals in the Old Testament and the sacrifice of Jesus in the New Testament. How many times did Jesus get crucified? One. This tells us something utterly comforting. The sacrifice, the substitutionary atonement, the payment was **permanent**. No longer does a sacrifice need to be made once a year involving tons of specific details. When Jesus went to the cross, He made a final declaration seen in John 19:30. "It is finished." This ordinance is not lasting. It is final! No longer are we guilty. No longer are we in debt. The price has been paid, and thank God, it is permanent.

How can this be? What makes Jesus so different? What makes His sacrifice so permanent? Adam and Eve's introductory sin brought forth the consequences we have already talked about. One of those consequences was the requirement of a **perfect** sacrifice. The only way to fully pay for our sin, and the only way to satisfy the wrath of God is to sacrifice perfection. None of us were qualified. We have all sinned (Romans 3:23). Since no one was perfect, we were hopeless to have a restored relationship with God. The only perfect being in the universe is the One that created it. Since God was the only One qualified, He had enough love to show the greatest love. He had enough love that He sent Himself, in the form of Jesus, to make the perfect payment that was required. If the propitiation were not perfect, it would not have been permanent. How grateful are you that it was? This is what makes Jesus the ultimate sacrifice. He claimed that the greatest way to reveal His love was to lay down one life for another. He taught it, He practiced it, and He finally showed it in full form. When Jesus went to the cross, He put us before Himself. He chose *us* and laid down His perfect life for *us*! This is the true essence of the beauty of what a sacrifice represents.

MAKING THE CONNECTION

One of the most valuable ideas I took hold of while getting my degree in education at Berry College was the aspect of transferable data. I was a physical education major, so I was taught the idea in the setting of sports skills. Here is an example. If I were trying to teach a student how to serve a tennis ball, I would tell them the motion is kind of like serving in volleyball. The object used to strike the ball is different, but the motion is quite similar. If I were teaching a student how to kick a football correctly, I would tell them the motion is similar to the way they would kick a soccer ball. I take knowledge from something they know and simply place it in a new setting. Like I said, this is a valuable tool for teaching, and teachers everywhere are likely to use this tactic. This concept is easy to see in the setting of sports and games, but it can also be used with any other topic.

    Having that said, I am going to come back to the topic of my mother being a woman of great sacrifice. As I mentioned like a broken record before, my mother was always and still remains one of the selfless people I know. She was constantly putting others first and considering them better than herself. Her whole life was about laying down her life for others. As I also mentioned before, she taught me this priceless lesson through the tactic of demonstration. Monkey see, monkey do. That is probably the best way to describe it. My whole life, my mom was showing me how to sacrifice myself for others. This is valuable, but she was actually showing me something even more important.

When I started getting older reaching high school and college, I began to comprehend the idea of Jesus being our ultimate sacrifice. I started realizing everything I wrote in the last section about Jesus. I learned how the greatest way Jesus showed His love for me was by laying down His life for me. Then I had an epiphany that changed my life. Here was my thought: "It's kind of like the way my mom always put us before herself." The more I processed that thought, the more I began to notice that my mother was doing so much more than showing me how to put others first. My mother was actually showing me Jesus! I realized that the reason I was able to easily understand the concept of Jesus being a sacrifice was because my mother was showing me that very concept my entire life. I had the knowledge; it was simply a matter of transferring the knowledge to a different setting. Have you heard of the idea that it is hard for people to see God as a father if their earthly father was not really there for them? It's all about a transfer of knowledge. It is hard to transfer something from one setting to another if you did not have any knowledge to begin with. If the student in my previous example did not already know how to kick a soccer ball, the transferring tool would have been useless. It is basically the same concept. It was so simple for me to see something that I was already being shown for so long. I am so grateful for the way my mother consistently put us before herself because, without noticing, she was making God more tangible for me and for anyone she came into contact with. She was equipping us with knowledge that we would later be able to transfer. I love how God set that up!

ONE PERSON, TWO SELVES

Do you know anyone in your life or maybe someone you see on a consistent basis that is completely selfish? I'm talking about the people who always have to be right, always have to be the center of attention, or always have to have things go *their* way. Do you know any people like this? You know what they say…if you don't know any people like this, you probably are one. I always find those sayings humorous, but that is mostly because they are usually true. However, here is some comfort for those of you who aren't really sure if you are this person or not. We are ALL those people! We are all selfish at some point in our lives. Here is how I know this to be true. I am a strong believer that all sin stems from selfishness. I know absolutes tend to freak people out, but I stand by my claim. ALL sin is rooted with selfishness. Seeing as how Paul correctly declares, "all have sinned," in his letter to the Romans, it is safe to say that we have all been selfish. Let me make my point by taking a look at the Ten Commandments. Why do people lie? They don't want to get **themselves** in trouble. Why do some men cheat on their wives? They are seeking pleasure for **themselves**. Why do we covet? We want what others have for **ourselves.** Sin is rebelling against God and rebelling against God is saying, "**My** way is better." To wrap up, if you have been selfish, you have probably sinned in that selfishness no matter how subtle it may be. Think about Jesus. Nothing about Him was selfish. He came to seek and to save the lost (Luke 19:10). His coming really had nothing to do with what *He* was going to get. His coming had everything to do with what He was going to give.

Now, I had to make that point clear before coming to my main point. When we are selfish, we usually fall into sin. When we sin, we become separated from God. If you are separated from God, it is going to be extremely difficult to see, hear, or feel God the way you were created to. Did you follow me? Ultimately, It is much harder for God's presence to be felt in our lives when we are being selfish. This is why so many of us are failing to see God the way we want to. We do not see Him as tangible because we are being blinded by our own selfishness.

Let's take a look at the opposite end of the spectrum. Look at what happens when we become self*less*. When you are selfless, you are putting others before yourself. When you put others before yourself, you are showing love. When you show love, you show every essence of God's character. We have already seen that when we love, we are making God more tangible. Therefore, He becomes much easier for us to see. As a result, when we practice selflessness, we are making God more visible for someone else. So let's review. When we are selfish, we sin and separate ourselves from God. This makes it hard to see God. When we are selfless, we love and connect with God. This makes it easy to see God.

This is exactly what we are doing when we sacrifice and lay down our lives for our friends. When we put the interests of others before our own interests, we are showing love of the highest kind. This is how my mother made the love of Jesus so tangible and real for my siblings and me. She constantly laid down her life by putting us first. She was completely selfless. Can you imagine a parent that always puts their own interests ahead of their children's?

FINDING YOURSELF

It is completely possible for us to see God in a real and tangible way. The power, however, lies in us. If you want to see, hear, or feel the presence of God more in your life, try taking the road that will lead you there. When you lay down your life for someone else, it may be hard to see at first, but *you* are the one receiving the greatest reward. Though you feel like you have received the short end of the stick, you have just opened up an opportunity to connect with God in a way you never have before. The best way to receive life is, ironically, to lay down your life. When this happens, you are doing exactly what Jesus did. It is amazing how much closer you feel to Jesus when you put yourself in His shoes. The opportunities are everywhere for us to show God's love by laying down our lives for the sake of others. We understand the concept because most of us have been shown this love throughout our lives. It is simply a matter of transferring the knowledge to the appropriate setting. When we fully comprehend the selfless love Jesus showed us, we will be fully able to show the selfless love of Jesus. It is impossible to keep God from revealing Himself when this happens.

When I was working as a student athletic trainer in college, we had a quote we lived by every time we step into the training room. "We find ourselves when we lose ourselves in the service of others." What incredible truth spoken here! When you finally have that powerful encounter with God, it is like everything begins to make sense. You start realizing exactly why you were put here. In a way, when you find God, you are able to find yourself because you find your purpose. How do we find God? We make Him more visible by "losing ourselves" in the service of others.

Chapter 11

The Power Within
It may take looking in the mirror to see God.

I had a student make the comment one time that they did not believe in God because He was not tangible. You could not see Him, hear Him, or feel Him. This very comment is actually the motivation that is driving me to write this book. This student is not alone. Many of us have this same belief. Even though some of us may have been following Jesus for many years now, there are still times when we wished we could see or hear Him better. It is a struggle we all tend to deal with from time to time. I did try to communicate a particular idea to this student that I will also try to use in this chapter. Many pastors and teachers have used this analogy, but it is the best picture I have found to make this point. I think it helped this teenager see God in a different way, and hopefully, it will do the same for you.

IT'S NOT JUST THE WIND

Is the wind real? I'm really not trying to insult your intelligence. Is it tangible? Like my young student, some of us may be inclined to respond with a resounding yes. Think about it. Can you see the wind? Again, you may be tempted to affirm that you can, but the scientific truth is that the wind is invisible. No one can physically see the wind. The only way wind is made visible is by the objects it moves through. You cannot actually see the wind, but you can see the waves of the ocean. You can see the leaves dancing on a tree. You can see the clouds racing across the sky. You can even see and feel the hairs on your own head trying to escape. The wind is only made visible when it is moving in something else. On the other end of the spectrum, the objects are not going to move without the wind. Waves will not form in the ocean without the wind. The leaves will stand still without the wind. Have you ever found yourself giving someone else the command "look at the wind"? It is something that is invisible, yet no one will hesitate to proclaim the reality of the wind's presence. It is an intangible force that makes itself tangible through other things.

My goal of this entire book is to show that God can be looked at the same way. God is currently an intangible being that makes Himself tangible through other things. He is invisible yet revealing Himself at the same time. How is this possible? The same way it's possible with the wind. When God moves and makes Himself active, objects are affected. One of the differences with God and the wind is that, in God's scenario, *we* are the objects being affected. We are the water and the leaves that God uses to reveal Himself. God is constantly using His creations to reveal Himself to us. The problem, however, is that some of us are simply failing to notice.

BEAUTIFULLY INADEQUATE

I can still remember the first sermon I ever preached on a Sunday morning. I had just finished my junior year in college and was serving in the church over the summer. The lead pastor came up to me and told me that I was going to preach at least one Sunday morning. I started sweating bullets. I had a little experience speaking to teenagers, but I had never taken on the monster of "big church". I agreed and said I'd just worry about it when the time came. The truth is, I had no idea what I was being thrown into. The series was called "Unstoppable", and I was teaching on love. So here

I am. A single college student who has never been engaged or married, and I have to teach the entire church about what true love is. Can you imagine how unworthy I felt? I had no idea what I was talking about, and frankly, I had no authority to say anything. Somehow, through the fumbling of my words, there were a couple people who had a true encounter with Jesus that morning.

Have you ever felt unworthy or inadequate? Maybe somebody asked you to do something that you knew you were incapable of doing. If nothing comes to mind, put yourself in my shoes. What if your pastor came up to you tomorrow morning and asked you to give the message on Sunday. Like myself, most of us may be hesitant at first because we feel like we don't have enough knowledge, ability, or authority.

"Who am I to do something like that? God, you need to pick someone more worthy. Did you say *my* name, God? Are you sure you know what you are requesting?"

Isn't it funny how often we forget the character of God? We are still so surprised when He calls the weak to do something strong. The character of God is never going to change; that we can count on. Think back over every story you have heard of God using someone in the Bible. Has He *ever* used the person that was most qualified to accomplish His will? Let's take a walk down memory lane.

Have you ever heard of Moses? God used Moses to deliver the Israelites out of slavery. Moses is commonly referred to as having been the mouthpiece of God. Moses spoke with authority to Pharaoh and inflicted ten plagues on an entire nation of people. He also stuck his staff into the Red Sea and had it divide perfectly so his people could cross on dry ground. Moses led thousands of people away from slavery and towards their Creator. Do you recall Moses' response to God in their first conversation?

> *"Who am I that I should go to Pharaoh and bring the children of Israel out of Egypt?"*
> Exodus 3:11 (ESV)

Do you remember David? David was a boy that became a man when he overcame a giant to free his people. David became one of the greatest kings of Israel. Jesus, God in the flesh, descended from the house of David. This is a pretty big honor. Where did it all start?

> *And Saul said to David, "You are not able to go against this Philistine to fight with him, for you are but a youth, and he has been a man of war from his youth."*

1 Samuel 17:33 (ESV)

We cannot mention unworthiness without bringing up Paul. Paul is only the author of most of the books in the New Testament. Paul suffered more than anyone, but advanced the gospel of Christ above all costs. He did wondrous things for God's kingdom, and one cannot think of love without thinking about Paul's words to the Corinthians. How did Paul's journey start again?

> *But Ananias answered, "Lord, I have heard from many about this man, how much evil he has done to your saints at Jerusalem. And here he has authority from the chief priests to bind all who call on your name."*

Acts 9:13-14 (ESV)

Moses was an orphan with a stuttering problem. David was an undersized shepherd boy that was far outmatched. Paul was a ruthless murderer who persecuted Christ. None of these men had resumes that made them worthy of accomplishing God's will. I only used three examples, but the Bible is full of stories where God used the most unlikely person to do something incredible. God has a way of always using the inadequate. It is as if our weakness is a requirement rather than a hindrance.

As a reminder, God is in the business of glorifying Himself. If any of those three men were actually worthy of achieving such feats, the credit would have been falsely assigned. People would be singing praises to Moses, David, or Paul rather than to God. No. God made sure that He was the only One capable of receiving the credit for what was happening. The reason our inadequacy is so beautiful is that it clearly throws all the glory in God's direction. Our unworthiness shouts that God is the only explanation.

Paul writes about his own weaknesses in his second letter to the Corinthians, and not only does he admit his faults, he goes further and brags about them.

> *But he said to me, "My grace is sufficient for you, for my power is made perfect in*

weakness." Therefore I will boast all the more gladly of my weaknesses, so that the power of Christ may rest upon me. For the sake of Christ, then, I am content with weaknesses, insults, hardships, persecutions, and calamities. For when I am weak, then I am strong.

2 Corinthians 12: 9-10 (ESV)

God's power is made perfect in our weakness. What does this mean? It means when we do something we are unworthy of doing, God is made transparent in us. His work is manifested in us. Paul is boasting about his weaknesses and faults because every ounce of his inadequacy points us straight to God. The apostle understood that God was using Paul's weaknesses to reveal Himself. Do you see how Paul felt honored to be used by God through his faults? Here is what Paul was trying to convey with his profound statement. When we accomplish the impossible, it points to the only One who has the authority to make the impossible possible. None of us are qualified to be used by God, but this is a good thing. It is purely good because God ends up with all the credit. The weaker we are, the more God is seen and glorified when the impossible happens.

THE UNWORHTY TWELVE

One of the most intriguing groups of people in history were the disciples of Jesus. These men were basically Jesus' shadow. It was like "bring-your-disciple-to-work day" twelve times over. Every day. You would think the people who spent the most time with Jesus would be the most educated about Jesus, but let's be honest. These men were not exactly the sharpest tools in the shed. I use this characterization loosely because, in their defense, anyone would seem a little slow when standing next the One who is all-knowing. It's also easier for us to look back and critique events that have already happened. I'm sure I would have definitely asked some of the same questions Peter asked. Nonetheless, there are a couple times when the dozen's "human tendencies" show their face. One example is found in John's gospel. Jesus is sitting with His disciples at the last supper, which means it is nearing the end of their time together. At this point, they have seen Jesus do so many miraculous things, they've heard every message He has given, and they have been taught so much about

His true identity. They have learned so much! They are ready to go and teach! Then, they open their mouths. Look at the dialogue here:

> [7] *If you had known me, you would have known my Father also. From now on you do know him and have seen him."*
>
> [8] *Philip said to him, "Lord, show us the Father, and it is enough for us." [9] Jesus said to him, "Have I been with you so long, and you still do not know me, Philip? Whoever has seen me has seen the Father. How can you say, 'Show us the Father'? [10] Do you not believe that I am in the Father and the Father is in me?*
>
> John 14:7-10 (ESV)

Was Philip absent or late the first day of class when they went over this? Jesus explains it pretty well in verse seven where most of us would probably catch on to what He was saying. Right after Jesus completes His statement about Him and the Father being one, Philip comes in.

"Wait, wait, wait, wait, wait… now *who* is the Father?"

I can just sense Jesus' mannerisms when Philip asked this fundamental question. I can see His head drop instantly with his hand over His eyes. Jesus' reaction is quite perfect as He gently reminds Philip of His identity. I poke at Philip here, but again, this was an idea that was, and still is, extremely hard for us to grasp.

Another interesting moment where the disciples' simplemindedness shined through involved Peter. Jesus had just defeated death by rising from the dead, and some of his faithful friends were doing what they did best, fishing. In John 21, Jesus calls out to them asking if they had caught anything with some additional advice on how to improve their results. Once Peter finds out the man on the shore is Jesus, he tries to get to him as quickly as possible. So, what does he do? He jumps into the water and starts swimming to shore. Is it just me, or does it seem like *swimming* a hundred yards is not exactly the fastest way to get across a lake? Wouldn't the boat have been the faster choice? I feel like this would be the same as getting out of a car and running down the highway in hopes of getting to your destination quicker.

Now, there *is* a beautiful passion we see in Peter when he jumps ship. It shows his willingness to do whatever it takes to get to Christ. I'm simply using this story to show that when Jesus was actually *with* the disciples, they did not have the best record of making the wisest decisions. Jesus used parables many times to try to explain certain ideas, and then, He would have to go back and explain the actual parables because the twelve never really caught on.

I'm not trying to paint the disciples as idiots, but do you see how "human" they were? They felt just as inadequate as you and me. They were trying to figure the whole Jesus thing out just like we are trying to do. This group consisted of fishermen, tax collectors, doubters, etc. If you think they had flaws, you would be spot on. If you have ever felt a sense of unworthiness, you would be able to relate to these men. I know it sounds redundant, but we must grasp the reality of their weaknesses before moving on.

THE WORTHY TWELVE

Towards the end of Jesus' time on Earth, He shares a promise with His, now eleven, disciples. Jesus knew, better than anyone, how much help these men were going to need if *they* were going to be the ones to start building the church. He promises them a Helper for the first time in John 14. He then reminds them of that promise as His last piece of wisdom before ascending into heaven. This is specifically what Jesus says.

> *[8] But you will receive power when the Holy Spirit has come upon you, and you will be my witnesses in Jerusalem and in all Judea and Samaria, and to the end of the earth."*
>
> Acts 1:8 (ESV)

Soon after this, they brought their number back to a solid twelve with the addition of Matthias. Can you imagine the anticipation these guys were feeling? God in human form just told you that He was going to give you the very thing you need to do what He called you to do. As usual, however, He did not give them the exact hour that this would occur. Luke did not give many specifics about how long the time was, but some time after their last sight of Jesus, all the disciples were gathered together at Pentecost. Let's look at what happened.

> *Without warning there was a sound like a strong wind, gale force—no one could tell*

> *where it came from. It filled the whole building. Then, like a wildfire, the Holy Spirit spread through their ranks, and they started speaking in a number of different languages as the Spirit prompted them.*

Acts 2:2-4 (MSG)

As we have already discussed, these men were not the most educated men in the world, so they were definitely not multi-lingual. Then all of a sudden, they were speaking in tongues. We know they were not merely babbling because Luke shares with us later on in the chapter that a crowd came flocking to the scene. This crowd was extremely diverse and from all over the world, yet each language was accounted for. In verse 8, the people ask, "How is it that each of us hears them in his own native language?" Then, again in verse 11, they cry, "We hear them declaring the wonders of God in our own tongues!"

If you were able to grasp how unworthy these men were in the last section, you will definitely understand the significance of this event. This was huge! It was the first miracle the people had seen after Jesus ascended. It was the first time the people were able to see God's divine intervention manifested in these twelve men. In an instant, they went from ordinary to extraordinary through the power of God's Holy Spirit. Later on, in the third chapter of Acts, Peter and John are headed up to the temple when they run into a crippled beggar. Peter claims that he does not have anything physical to give the man, but he does have *something* to give him. Like a stud and with all the confidence in the world, Peter commands, "In the name of Jesus Christ of Nazareth, walk." After being helped up, the man then begins to walk and jump around praising God.

Do you see the incredible shift here? The guy who just healed a crippled beggar with simple words was the same guy who denied Jesus three consecutive times. It was the same guy who jumped out of the boat like a child. It was the same ordinary fisherman that nobody really noticed before. Peter, in an instant, went from dud to stud! How could this have happened? What made this unworthy fisherman now worthy to be able to speak in tongues, heal, and proclaim the Word of God like Solomon? If you are asking these questions, you can relate with everyone else that were actually witnessing these events. The people were bewildered and seeking answers to the madness when Peter then stepped up and quoted the prophet, Joel. Pay attention to these words because it is the motivation behind this entire chapter. This explanation Peter gave tells us exactly how these inadequate disciples now had the power of God. Here is what he says:

> *"'And in the last days it shall be, God declares,*
> *that I will pour out my Spirit on all flesh,*
> *and your sons and your daughters shall prophesy,*
>   *and your young men shall see visions,*
>   *and your old men shall dream dreams;*
> [18] *even on my male servants and female servants*
>   *in those days I will pour out my Spirit,*
> *and they shall prophesy.*
> [19] *And I will show wonders in the heavens above*
>   *and signs on the earth below,*
>   *blood, and fire, and vapor of smoke;*
> [20] *the sun shall be turned to darkness*
>   *and the moon to blood,*
>   *before the day of the Lord comes, the great and magnificent day.*

²¹ And it shall come to pass that everyone who calls upon the name of the Lord shall be saved.'

Acts 2:17-21 (ESV)

Something that is worth pointing out is that these disciples were the same men they were before. Peter did not turn into Jesus. He was still Peter. Matthew was still Matthew, and John was still John. Everything about Peter was the exact same as before, except one. There is one fundamental, yet enormous difference that explains his new abilities. The only denominator that changed was the presence of the Holy Spirit. Without the Helper, Peter was the ordinary fisherman. With the Helper, he was the extraordinary church leader. The presence of the Holy Spirit is the only explanation of how these unworthy men became worthy.

GOD IN US

Francis Chan wrote a book titled Forgotten God. Throughout his book, he does a fantastic job explaining the significance of the Holy Spirit in our lives. If you want a much deeper understanding of the Holy Spirit, it is definitely a book I recommend. One of my favorite parts about his book, however, is the title. As Christians, we are waiting in anticipation for Jesus to come back to us. We are waiting until we get to stand before God. We are eagerly longing for the time to come when we can be with God. These are good things, but have we forgotten that we have complete access to God right now? We seem to forget the potential we have to experience God every day we wake up.

The trinity is always hard to explain perfectly, but here is a way that has helped me in the past. There was always God the Father, God the Creator, God the Deliverer. Then comes Jesus, and people called Him Emmanuel. This term means "God with us." It perfectly describes how God was in human form living among us as Jesus. The part of God we forget about may be the most significant part of God in our day. When Jesus left, God was no longer *with* us. Jesus actually explains that this is better for us for Him to go because, unless He died and paid for sin, we would never be able to be reconciled to God. So, as we saw at Pentecost, the Holy Spirit comes once Jesus ascends into heaven. Since the disciples were now able to do things with the power of the Holy Spirit that Jesus did, we can refer to the Holy Spirit as "God in us." Isn't it crazy how God has always had a plan to reveal Himself to us? He has always made Himself available to His creations. It may be in various forms according to the context, but we have always had access to Him. Think about that for a minute.

The fact that Peter and the other disciples were filled with the Holy Spirit meant that God was now inside them. Before you start picturing a horror film involving aliens, let me clear this up. Peter had no authority and no power to be able to heal any man. Only God had the power to turn something that is dead to life. Only God can heal the broken. If God is the only One who had the power to heal, and Peter healed a man, the only conclusion we can arrive at is the fact that God made His power manifest in Peter. God was the One who healed. Peter was the tool in which God used. If a baseball player hits a homerun, God is the hitter, and Peter is the bat. The bat never gets the credit for hitting the homerun. All the glory goes to the hitter. The bat was simply a tool used to get the job done.

There is something amazing to think about when it comes to God using us. God does not need us to get the job done. He created the universe without a single helping hand, and He could heal anyone without picking up a tool at all. He has the authority to do whatever He wants to however He wants to do it. This brings us to one amazing truth. God does not *need* to use us; He *wants* to use us! Congratulations, you're a tool! I know that sounds offensive, but on a more serious note, think about the fact that God wants to reveal His work, reveal His power, reveal His will, and reveal Himself through…US! What greater honor is there? Check out how Paul explains it in his letter to the Colossians.

> *You have been given fullness in Christ, who is the head over every power and authority.*
> Colossians 2:10 (ESV)

We have been given fullness in Christ! The power that dwelt in Jesus can now dwell in us through the power of the Holy Spirit. Peter was able to heal the way Jesus healed. He was now able to speak the way Jesus spoke. The only similarity in these two men was the presence of God. Jesus *was* God, and Peter now had God inside of him.

YOU CAN DO IT

As I bring this back to where we are sitting today, think about your specific setting or circle of influence. Think about your job, your friends, or your family. What if God wanted to reveal Himself to everyone around you using...you? What if He wanted to reveal Himself through you the way He revealed Himself through Peter?

One thing we all have in common with the disciples pre-Pentecost is the fact that we are all unworthy. None of us have the authority to raise the dead to life. None of us have the power to save. We are all inadequate. Before you get offended and throw this book across the room, let us remember what we have already learned. When we are inadequate, we are in the perfect position for God to use us. Why? Because He knows the only explanation will be Him. All the glory has no other place to go but His direction.

The bad news is that there is nothing we can do to make us worthy. So many of us are lost because we are using the wrong map to try and get to our desired destination. We are trying to find our worth in things that will never be able to provide it. The good news, however, is that there is nothing we *have* to do to become worthy. God gave us Himself as a gift. Because Jesus died, paid our sin-caused debt, and was raised back to life, we can be reconciled back to God forever. Forever does not have to start when your body dies. Forever can start today. Right now! You can be reconciled to God today! When we are finally reconciled to God, it means that He gives us the greatest gift we could ever receive. He gives us the most valuable thing and gives us immeasurably more than anything we could ever ask for. There is incredible irony in this truth. Think about it. When we surrender, go to God, and finally confess our unworthiness, He actually gives us the very thing that makes us worthy. He gives us Himself. He gives us His Holy Spirit. The Holy Spirit is not an "it." The Holy Spirit is a "He," and His name is Yahweh. His name is Jesus. His name is Father. His name is God.

We don't understand the power that is within us. We are usually waiting for God to do something powerful inside of us, but what if God is the One waiting? If you are a follower of Christ, you have the Holy Spirit. If you have the Holy Spirit, you have God inside of you. If God is inside of you, there is an opportunity for God to come out of you. What this means is that, as a follower of Christ, every day you wake up is an opportunity to make God tangible for someone else. The reason God is the One that is made tangible is because, as we have already discussed, we are naturally sinful.

It doesn't come natural for us to selflessly lay down our lives and our desires for someone else. The beauty in our inadequacy is the fact that when we *are* actually called to put someone else ahead of our selves, the glory is naturally going back to God. I am unworthy of loving the way Jesus did, but if I have the Holy Spirit, I am fully equipped to do so.

God may not be fully tangible, but we are. When we let God in and allow Him to reveal Himself through us, we are making Him more visible for someone else. We are making Him more noticeable by making His character fully tangible. So how do we allow God to reveal Himself through us? How do we make God more tangible for someone else? We show them His character. When you show someone forgiveness, they have the chance to see God's forgiveness. When you share your story with someone, they have the opportunity to see God's power. When you sacrifice yourself for someone else's sake, there is an opening for them to truly see God's love.

How did God reveal Himself to *you*? When did you truly see Him? Was it because you were shown His love through someone else? Was it because God showed you the truth through the obedience and preparation of a pastor? He could have been revealed to you in a number of different ways, but somehow, the reality of God became tangible for you in the form of someone else. What we need to understand is that, through the Holy Spirit, we have the same power and opportunity to show someone else exactly what we were shown. As soon as we truly saw God for the first time, we were given the ability to show Him to someone else. We spend too much time waiting around. Take what He has already given you (Himself), and show it to someone else. Again, maybe God is the One waiting on us. Maybe all He wants in order to reveal Himself is a willing heart.

One final thing we need to understand is that we cannot give something that we do not have. If the reality of God has never been revealed to you, there is no chance in showing it to someone else. The good news? You can be equipped today. In confessing your sinful nature and your unworthiness, you can be made new. You can experience the same instantaneous change the disciples experienced once they were given the Holy Spirit. For those of you that are already following Jesus, you have exactly what you need. Please don't waste another opportunity to make the reality of God known to someone else. Ask God to open up your eyes to notice the opportunities set before you. How can an intangible God become more tangible in our lives? Although it may take the form of poor in spirit, meekness, emptiness, or humility, the power may just be within you.

Chapter 12

The Way
It may take looking at the Son to see the Father.

Have you ever wondered why it is so difficult for us to see God? The reason we feel so far and disconnected from God and the reason it is so hard for us to see God is because of sin. You can call it our "mistakes" or come up with another feel-good term to make it seem better, but we are all covered in sin. The first thing Adam and Eve did after disobeying God was hide. They felt guilt, shame, and embarrassment, and because of this, they were separated from God. They were *with* God before sin and separated from God after sin. Being apart from God is the very thing blurring our vision and blinding us to His reality. The most tragic truth in the universe is the fact that we have acquired the same rebellious nature of Adam and Eve. It is this very nature that separates us from the God we were meant to be with. Ever since the fall in the third chapter of Genesis, we have been hopelessly trying to find our way back to Him. I know it sounds it all sounds discouraging, but there is light at the end of the tunnel. The beauty in the midst of this tragedy is that there *is* a way back. One thing we must understand, however, is that this way is very specific. There is no other way around this way. There is only one way that leads us back to Him. There is only one way we can see God the way we were meant to see Him. There is only one way to get back home.

One of the most well known stories in the Bible is the story of God delivering the Israelites out of Egypt. If you have never read the story, you have probably heard about it or watched it if you have ever seen "The Prince of Egypt." It is found in the early chapters of the book of Exodus if you would like to read the entire story, but I will simply be paraphrasing. The Israelites were enslaved in Egypt for 400 years when they cried out to God for help. As a response, God raised up a deliverer in Moses to set the people free. Pharaoh obviously wasn't on board because this meant losing all of his workers. When you oppose God's will, it usually means consequences are sure to follow. Pharaoh's circumstance was no different. In response to Pharaoh's hardened heart, God sent ten plagues overwhelming the land of Egypt. All ten plagues are listed in Exodus, chapter 10, but I would like to focus primarily on the last plague.

The last plague was the death of all the firstborn children in Egypt. Just like the rest of the plagues, this one was inevitable for anyone living in the land. Ironically enough, God *did* create a loophole for this plague; He provided a way to escape death for all the Israelites. He also gave them very specific instructions on how to be spared. Each family had to get a lamb for the week. They couldn't get just any ordinary lamb; among some other specifics, it had to be perfect and without blemish. Then, on the night that the plague would take effect, they were to slaughter the perfect lamb and wipe the blood over their doorposts. When God passed through that night to carry on with His promise to kill all the firstborn, if the sign of the blood of the perfect lamb was on the doorpost, the family would be spared from death and given life. The only escape from death for the Israelites was through the sacrifice of the perfect lamb. The lamb was the only way to life. This chapter is about that lamb.

FULLY GOD

If you are a Christian, there is something incredibly unique about your faith. There are actually many things that make what you believe different from every other faith in the world, but we are going to focus on the Everest of these differences. What comes to mind when you hear the name Jesus? Your definition of this name defines your faith. It defines everything you believe in. Most faiths refer to Jesus as a good teacher, and I would agree with them. Most faiths consider him a respectable and moral man, and I would agree. Although I agree with the goodness of Jesus, it tears me apart to know how overlooked His true identity is. He wasn't just a good teacher or a rabbi or a great community service leader. He is everything! Labeling Jesus with anything less than what He is causes an avalanche of meaning. Jesus did not fail to tell us who He was. If He was not who He said He was, the true meaning of love crumbles, and justice and grace go down the drain. If Jesus was not who He said He was, He becomes just a lying fool on a cross, and we are inevitably doomed. Do you see how everything rests on who He is? His identity defines the fate of the world.

On that beautiful morning, two days after Jesus' death, His true identity became clear. Friday meant nothing without Sunday. When He came back to life, eternity was sealed. When the tomb opened, love, justice, and grace were confirmed along with His true identity. When Jesus took His second, first breath, He showed the world that He was exactly who He was claiming to be. He finally, tangibly revealed to the world that He was so much more than the label they gave Him. He was more than a teacher, a rabbi, or a prophet. He was even more than simply the *Son* of God. Finally, Jesus revealed Himself as God in the flesh.

As soon as Jesus' identity was confirmed, everything He was talking about made sense. There are a couple reasons I want to point out why it makes complete sense that Jesus was in fact, God in human form. The first reason is simple. He could perform miracles and heal with authority. This is so overseen, but think about it. Before Jesus ascended into heaven, there was no Holy Spirit inside of us. The world had never seen a human heal the way Jesus healed. Yes, God empowered Moses to part the Red Sea, but Jesus was definitely set apart. He spoke people from death to life! Do you remember chapter 5 about nature? We learned that the only

One who can break the laws of nature is the author of nature. It is the same way with life. The only One who has the authority to take life or give it is the author of life itself. Let us refresh our memory from Genesis 1: In the beginning, God created_____. You can fill in the blank with whatever you want, and it fits. If God is the only One with the authority to give life, and Jesus spoke Lazarus, among others, to life, we must conclude that Jesus had the same authority as God. When Jesus calmed the storm in Matthew 8, the disciples started to notice His true character with their statement, "…even the winds and sea obey Him." All of nature obeys Jesus because Jesus is God, and He is the only One who has the authority to command nature as He pleases.

The next reason goes back to the lamb. The only way the Israelites could escape death was through the requirement of a perfect blood sacrifice in the lamb. If you haven't caught on yet, that is exactly why we refer to Jesus as the lamb. It's not because lambs are sweet, nice, and cuddly. It's because Jesus fits the same role as the perfect blood sacrifice. Because of our sin, we have earned death (Romans 6:23), and the debt is too much for us to pay. The only way our debt could be paid was through the requirement of a perfect blood sacrifice. The payment had to be perfect because only perfection could make the payment permanent. Remember the saying, "Nobody's perfect?" It's true. This truth is what gave us the characteristic of being hopelessly sinful. We are hopeless because, as we learned in the last chapter, none of us are able to make a payment that is worthy enough to pay for sin.

I know that sounds discouraging, but the fact that we are hopeless is what makes the story so sweet. The only thing we can associate with perfection is God. He is the only perfect being. Ever. Since perfection was the only way to cover the payment of sin, God was the only One worthy of making the payment. That is exactly what He did. Being the only One capable, God became a human, and His name was Jesus. If Jesus was the only perfect human to ever exist, we've already concluded that the only thing that can be associated with perfection is God. This also goes back to our simple equation. If only God is perfect, and only Jesus is perfect, then only Jesus is God. The first chapter of John's gospel actually describes it pretty well.

1 In the beginning was the Word, and the Word was with God, and the Word was God. ² He was in the beginning with God. ³ All things were made through him, and without him was not any thing made that was made. ⁴ In him was life and the life was the light of men. ⁵ The light shines in the darkness, and the darkness has not overcome it.

⁹ The true light, which gives light to everyone, was coming into the world. ¹⁰ He was in the world, and the world was made through him, yet the world did not know him. ¹¹ He came to his own, and his own people did not receive him. ¹² But to all who did receive him, who believed in his name, he gave the right to become children of God, ¹³ who were born, not of blood nor of the will of the flesh nor of the will of man, but of God.¹⁴ And the Word became flesh and dwelt among us, and we have seen his glory, glory as of the only Son from the Father, full of grace and truth.

John 1:1-5,9-14 (ESV)

In the beginning was the Word- First of all; we've already established in Genesis 1 that there was one person in the beginning. "In the beginning, God..." We also see that "Word" is capitalized which shows that it is a name. The only conclusion we can make from this sentence is that God is the Word.

The Word was with God, and the Word was God- with this statement, we begin to get a little confused because if the Word is God, why does it say the Word was *with* God? The only thing we can do is keep this in mind and keep reading. John then affirms what we've concluded so far. The Word was God, but we still have in the back of our minds that he intentionally stuck "with" in there. Let's continue.

The true light, which gives light to everyone, was coming into the world- who gave light to everyone? Again, Genesis 1 makes it clear. God was the One that created light. If God is the true light, then God was coming into the world. What a crazy thought! Let's keep going.

He was in the world- this makes it completely clear that God was in the world. God came to Earth.

He came to His own, and His own people did not receive Him- this shows that God has ownership over us, which makes complete sense seeing as how God created us. Then comes the most heart-breaking statement of all. We, His own people, did not receive Him. How was it that God left all of His glory, came down to our little planet, and we didn't even recognize Him? Does this sound bizarre to everyone else? I think the only explanation was that God did not look like what we expected Him to look like.

And the Word became flesh and dwelt among us, and we have seen his glory, glory as of the only Son from the Father, full of grace and truth- now we can definitely say that God became a human because we already learned that the Word was God. If the Word became flesh, God became flesh. God took the form of a human and dwelt among us. John is being extremely literal here when he says that we have seen the glory of God. He is saying that we have tangibly, visibly seen God's glory on Earth. He also shares that we have seen God's glory by means of the only Son from the Father, "full of grace and truth." I wanted to highlight those specific words because those words are later used to show us exactly who God was when He dwelt among us in human form. Pay close attention to this next verse because it explains and clears up every bit of confusion surrounding this text.

> *"...grace and truth came through Jesus Christ."*
>
> John 1:17 (ESV)

Do you understand the significance of this proclamation? We can tangibly see God's glory through grace and truth. Grace and truth came through Jesus Christ. When we label Jesus Christ as God, everything falls into place. If we know for a fact that God became flesh and dwelt among us as a human, the only human that fits is Jesus. God was the only perfect being. Jesus was the only perfect human. If was a human, He had to be Jesus.

Do you remember what we placed in the back of our minds a little bit ago? The Word was *with* God. We claimed that it made sense that God was the Word, but what if we aligned the Word with Jesus? *In the beginning was Jesus, and Jesus was with God, and Jesus was God. Jesus was in the beginning with God.* Let's skip down a little further still replacing "He" or "Word" with "Jesus." *Jesus was in the world, and the world was made through Him, yet the world did not know Him. Jesus came to His own, and His own people did not receive Him.* When you put Jesus' name in the last two sentences, it makes complete sense when you think about the way Jesus was treated. The religious people, the Pharisees, the Jews, all of them treated Jesus as if He was an outcast or an outsider. They refused to see Him as one of them. His own did not receive Him.

Every time you align Jesus with God, it fits perfectly. Every characteristic of Jesus revealed a characteristic of God. Every word of Jesus revealed the word of God. The grace and truth found in Jesus revealed the grace and truth established by God. Every time Jesus was glorified, God was glorified. When Jesus is God, love is so much sweeter because God left everything to die for us. When Jesus is God, grace is so much more amazing because of how we offended Him. When Jesus is God, justice is finally served because the price of sin is finally paid for. The only way our sins can be fully paid for is if Jesus was fully God.

FULLY HUMAN

One of the most overlooked concepts in our world is the idea that you can be two things while being one at the same time. I'm not getting into a deep discussion on the trinity; I'm talking about our everyday lives. You may think it is utterly impossible to have two different identities at the same time unless there is a medical issue, but this actually occurs more than we notice. Think about your parents. You see them as your parents, and that is exactly who they are. Did you ever think about the fact that while your parents are indeed parents, they are also a son and a daughter? The fact that your father is a father does not change the fact that he is a son as well. He is fully a father, and he is fully a son.

This same idea rests in the identity of Jesus. While we concluded that He was fully God, at the same time, He was fully human. We are going to dive deeper into the wonder of this truth in a minute, but we have to understand that Jesus was not merely half-man, half-God. The fact that Jesus was God took nothing away from how human He was. I know it sounds confusing, but this is the very thing that makes the gospel, the entire story, so beautiful. While Jesus was fully able to and had every bit of authority to raise a dead man to life, He was also fully capable of relating to you and me in every way possible. One of the best passages in the Bible that depicts both of Jesus' identities is found in Paul's letter to the Philippians. As we go through these descriptions of Jesus as a human, try to remember the section we just discussed and how Godly He actually was.

> *You must have the same attitude that Christ Jesus had. Though he was God, he did not think of equality with God as something to cling to.*
>
> Philippians 2:5-6 (NLT)

I had to start with this idea because it affirms everything we just discussed. Though Jesus was [fully] God, He did not consider Himself God. We immediately see how committed He was to His mission. This is the first sign of Jesus' human nature that He is showing us. We, as humans, will never be on the same level as God because His ways are so much higher than our ways (Isaiah 55:9). Jesus reveals how human He is that, while being God, did not consider equality with God even possible. There is so much goodness in this truth, and it's only the first verse in our journey. Let's keep digging.

> *Instead, he gave up his divine privileges; he took the humble position of a slave and was born as a human being. When he appeared in human form, he humbled himself in obedience to God and died a criminal's death on a cross.*
> Philippians 2:7-8 (NLT)

Jesus gave up His divine privileges. To make this statement more real, let's use Jesus' other name. God gave up His divine privileges. I love how the New International Version words it as it says, "Rather, He made Himself nothing." God could have made Himself a human and still ruled the world by taking the identity of a powerful king as the Jews were expecting, but He takes another route. He turns Himself into a human and takes the nature of a servant. A lot of us have heard this before and know it to be true, but let's allow this to truly sink in for a minute. The God who created every living thing simply by the words of His mouth, the God who knows every star by name and can hold the Pleiades in the palm of His hand, the

God who is bigger than anything our minds can comprehend, *this* God, chose to give it all up to learn how to walk. He left every bit of His glory and had to be potty-trained. He had to learn how to talk and strap on a sandal. He had to learn about the stars that He had already created and named. Are you getting the point? As much as Jesus was God, He was just as much human. This means everything you have had to learn to do, Jesus had to learn as well. If we had to learn how to eat, so did Jesus. The God who gave us the food to eat chose to leave His glory and learn how to eat the food He already provided. He was fully human.

This truth is amazing because of the fact that God made Himself truly tangible to us in the most physical way possible. He looked like a human and sounded like a human. Having a physical body, Jesus also experienced physical pain. He did not have to go through childbirth or deal with a broken bone, but I'd take those any day compared to what He went through. The point here is to see how much we can relate with Jesus when it comes to our physical bodies. The Word became flesh. God had skin, bones, muscles, and hair. When we go through physical pain, Jesus is able to say, "Yeah, I've been there. That doesn't feel good." When we get tired, we have a God who understands exactly how we feel. Without becoming fully human, this would not have been possible. There would always be a disconnect between God and us.

Another idea we tend to overlook is how much Jesus can relate to us in a nonphysical way. When God chose to become a human, in addition to physical compatibility, He took on everything we feel mentally, emotionally, and spiritually. This means Jesus can relate to us when we get irritated, when we feel anger, and when we get scared. He had the same emotions we have and yearned the same way we yearn. Every time you think you seem distant from God and feel alone in the depths of the pit that you're in, know that Jesus felt the exact same way hanging on the cross. Jesus is able to show impeccable empathy because He has walked where we walk and has felt as we feel. He put Himself in our shoes and can relate to us in every way imaginable. The author of Hebrews describes this truth flawlessly.

> *For we do not have a high priest who is unable to sympathize with our weaknesses, but one who in every respect has been tempted as we are, yet without sin. Let*

> *us then with confidence draw near to the throne of grace, that we may receive mercy and find grace to help in time of need.*
> Hebrews 4:15-16 (ESV)

When you're fasting and feel weak and hungry, Jesus has been there. When you are tempted to trade the ultimate for the immediate, Jesus has been there. When your closest friend stabs you in the back and betrays you, Jesus had been there. When you've worked insanely hard all week and desperately need some rest, Jesus has been there. Anything you feel on a daily basis, God is calling out to you shouting, "I've been there! I know it's tough. Tell me about it. I know exactly how you feel." As real and tangible as your physical and emotional pain is, God made Himself more tangible by feeling the same pain through Jesus Christ. This is what makes the story so beautiful. He left everything for our benefit. When Jesus became fully human, He connected us to God and to Himself for eternity.

THE SUM OF ALL

As soon as we find out about God, we spend our lives thinking about Him. Whether you choose to follow Him or not, we all choose our paths based on what we've seen or not seen. Even the most devout atheists were, at some point, informed about the mysteries of God. They simply chose not to believe based on what they failed to see. The problem does not lie in what we are trying to see; the problem is where we are looking. This is the very reason the religious leaders in Jesus' day failed to see God when He was walking right beside them. The problem did not rest in what they were looking for. They were seeking God. The problem was found in where they were looking. They were taught and knew a Messiah was coming. He just did not reveal Himself the way they were expecting. They were looking in palaces and castles when He was in a manger. They were looking at the healthy when He was with the sick. If you have had trouble seeing God in a real and tangible way, maybe your struggle isn't found in what you're trying to see. Maybe you've just spent too much time looking in the wrong places. The good news, however, is that the purpose of this book is to show us where to look to finally find what and who we are looking for.

Throughout this book, there have been eleven chapters revealing some sort of character of God. We have looked at how He speaks with us, how He calls us, how He loves us, how He seeks us, and so on. The goal was to show how the reality of God can be seen through everything we experience in each specific chapter. Hopefully, my efforts will help in getting us to a point where we can notice God more tangibly in every aspect of our lives. The reality, however, is that seeing God will still continue to be a struggle on a daily basis. When we're busy, when kids are screaming, when we are suffering in our lowest pits, when we are asked to sacrifice so much of ourselves, when life throws us in a whirlwind, it is going to get difficult for us to truly see God. There is an enemy who is fighting for your soul, and he is going to do whatever he can to distract you and blur your vision. He doesn't necessarily want us to worship him; he just doesn't want us to worship God. He is clever, though, because he knows that it gets hard to worship God when we can't see God.

So how can we fight against this enemy? We cling to the only thing that connects us to God. His name is Jesus. When you become burnt out and don't know where to look to find God, look at Jesus. When you get lost and don't know your way back, look at Jesus. When you aren't sure where to find love and acceptance, look at Jesus. He is the perfect picture of God and the only way back home. Everything Jesus was perfectly depicts every character of God.

Nice to Meet You: The way we see God through divine appointments is found in the way people had a real encounter with Jesus. He was intentional in meeting people where they were and revealing something better. Even when people heard about Jesus, their lives weren't changed until they had a real encounter with Him. The way Jesus pursued the lost reveals God's desire to pursue us. God was made tangible through the encounters Jesus had with people.

Good Teacher: When Jesus was teaching His students, He was revealing God's desire to offer us a better way. He taught in a way that made people want to learn and want to know more about Him. The way Jesus pushed His disciples to their limits shows God's yearning to see us grow and flourish. Because of how Jesus used every possible way to teach us more about Himself, we are able to see God in the teachable moments He gives us. God was made tangible through the way Jesus taught His students.

Competitive-Natured: When Jesus put together His team of disciples, He exposed God's plan in using each of our gifts to accomplish His will. God's power over Satan was tangibly revealed to us when Jesus stood up in the garden and crushed the head of the serpent. The way Jesus confidently proclaimed, "It is finished," and rose from the dead perfectly displayed God's ultimate victory. God was made tangible through the way Jesus fought for something great.

A Little More Conversation: When we look at how Jesus talked to God, we are shown the intimacy God seeks with all of us. The way Jesus lived a life of prayer revealed how God wants a constant relationship with us. When Jesus spoke to the people around Him, He allowed us to hear the gentle, firm, and loving voice of God. God was made tangible through every word that came out of Jesus' mouth.

Open the Blinds: When Jesus took His closest disciples to the top of Mount Sinai, we were able to see God's desire to show us His mighty work. The time Jesus was praying in the garden displayed how close we can get with God when we put ourselves in the midst of His creation. The way the North Star pointed the wise men straight to Jesus reflected how we are reminded directly of God when adoring His stars. God was made tangible through the way Jesus enjoyed every bit of God's creations.

Gone Fishing: The way Jesus was intentional in who He called to be His disciples revealed that God has a plan for each of us. The way Jesus approached certain people painted a picture of how God gently approaches us. With the great commission Jesus gave, He voiced God's desire to see us make disciples. God was made tangible through the way Jesus fished for His followers.

Do You Believe In Miracles: Every time Jesus healed someone, we witnessed the healing power of God. When Jesus brought Lazarus back to life, God's authority was made visible for us. When Jesus told people of future events, He demonstrated God's omniscient character. God was made tangible through the way Jesus made the impossible possible.

The Hill In The Race: When Jesus went through the immense suffering, He illustrated God's wrath because of our sin. The way Jesus endured through suffering displayed God's desire for us to persevere through the storms of life. God was made tangible through the way Jesus held on to Him in the midst of struggle.

The Simple Equation: God's love was perfectly seen in the way Jesus loved us. When Jesus rebuked the sins that held people captive, He showed God's love in freeing us from sin. When Jesus had mercy on those who mocked and cursed Him, He exhibited how God calls us to love our enemies. When Jesus commanded His disciples to love each other, God's voice was telling us to love each other. God was made tangible through the way Jesus showed love to everyone He came into contact with.

Lose Yourself: Because Jesus took our place on the cross, we were able to clearly see God's willingness to give Himself up for us. When Jesus died on the cross, we were shown the greatest love God could offer. The way Jesus put others first is the way God calls us to sacrifice ourselves for the sake of others. God was made tangible through the way Jesus innocently died on our behalf.

The Power Within: The way Jesus spoke about God demonstrated how we could speak about God with the help of the Holy Spirit. When Jesus did something extraordinary, He exposed God's desire to do extraordinary things through us. God was made tangible through the way Jesus allowed Himself to be used by God.

Every tangible way to see God was found in Jesus. Every time your vision is compromised, look to Jesus, and you will find the true character of God. The life of Jesus encompassed everything we yearn to see in God. When you find yourself asking for God to reveal how much He loves you, you will be pointed to the tangible picture of His Son taking your place on the cross. Take a look at the following verses that speak for themselves.

> *For in him the whole fullness of deity dwells bodily.*
>
> Colossians 2:9 (ESV)

> *He is the radiance of the glory of God and the exact imprint of his nature, and he upholds the universe by the word of his power. After making purification for sins, he sat down at the right hand of the Majesty on high.*
> Hebrews 1:3 (ESV)

> *He is the image of the invisible God, the firstborn of all creation. For by him all things were created, in heaven and on earth, visible and invisible, whether thrones*

> *or dominions or rulers or authorities—all things were created through him and for him. And he is before all things, and in him all things hold together. And he is the head of the body, the church. He is the beginning, the firstborn from the dead, that in everything he might be preeminent. For in him all the fullness of God was pleased to dwell, and through him to reconcile to himself all things, whether on earth or in heaven, making peace by the blood of his cross.*

Colossians 1:15-20 (ESV)

SHOW US THE FATHER

One thing that most theistic faiths have in common is their belief in God. Islam, Judaism, Mormonism, Jehovah's Witnesses, Christianity, and others have the belief that there is a higher power or One that is over all. There are different names assigned to this higher power and some characteristics change depending on which one you're associated with, but the overwhelming agreement is that this higher power does exist. Along with a belief in God naturally comes a yearning to eventually be with Him in some sort of paradise for eternity. We want to be able to see Him, talk to Him, and simply *be* with Him. The one question all of these faiths ask that shows their human similarity is this: How do we get to God? Finally, we arrive at the point of separation when it comes to every faith in the world. The answer to his question is what defines your faith, and in a way, defines your God. With so many different faiths in the world, you can see how people think that, as a result, there are many different ways to get to God. If there are so many ways to get to God, which way is best? This may be why so many people turn from God all together because they give up on trying to discern the best way to get to Him.

This question goes out to those who have given up or may be close to throwing in the towel. What if it wasn't supposed to be so complicated? What if there was only one true way to get to God, one way to see God, or one way to return to God? If you're a human, chances are you've wrestled with this predicament. How can I get to God? As we discussed in the first section of this chapter, there is one true way to get to God, and Jesus tells us exactly which way that is.

In John 14, Jesus takes the time to make it clear. His disciples are dealing with the very same issues we are dealing with today. They have heard all about this Father, this God, but how are they supposed to get to Him? In this passage, Jesus is calling out to everyone who is confused in how to get to God. How can we see God? Which way of all these ways is the right way? Thomas, who is also referred to as "Doubting Thomas," had doubts about which way to get to God. A lot of us can relate to Thomas' confusion when it comes to this topic. There are so many ways that are taught and so many directions that are given. How are we supposed to know the truth? Check out the conversation between Jesus and Thomas.

> *And you know the way to where I am going." Thomas said to him, "Lord, we do not know where you are going. How can we know the way?" Jesus said to him, "I am the way, and the truth, and the life. No one comes to the Father except through me. If you had known me, you would have known my Father also. From now on you do know him and have seen him."*
>
> John 14:4-7 (ESV)

In this one response, Jesus explains it all. "I am the way!" The only way to get back to God is through Jesus. The only way we can see God is through Jesus. The only way to tangibly spend eternity with God is through Jesus. Jesus proclaimed that He was THE way. There is no bad way or highway. There is one way and one way only to get to the Father. When Jesus took on the wrath of God on the cross and rose again, the gate opened, and we were given free and complete access to God for eternity. There is no chance of us getting to the Father if it's not through Jesus. This wrecks every other proposal, this closes every other road, and this trumps every other idea of how to get to God. Jesus was saying there is one door to get in to see God. Anybody can get in no matter what race, gender, age, weight, height, etc. There is no price you have to pay to get in, but there is only one way in. That way is through Jesus.

The disciples begin to understand this concept as we are, but they are still a little confused and have one more question that they want answered. They want to see the Father so passionately but have no idea where to look. They were hopelessly seeking as we are today. They know that Jesus is the *way* to the Father, but what about the Father Himself? Who is He? What does He look like? How will we know when we see Him? I know I was picking on Philip in the last chapter, but we have all been Philip at some point in our lives. In the eighth verse of John 14, Philip requested from Jesus, "Lord, show us the Father, and it is enough for us." If I could just see God, I would believe. If He would just give me a sign that He's really there, that would be enough for me to believe. If I could just hear Him talk, I would pray more and believe He's there. We all have this deep desire for God to reveal Himself to us in some way. We are all thinking it; Philip was just the one to bring it up. Here is Jesus' response to our popular request.

> *Jesus said to him, "Have I been with you so long, and you still do not know me, Philip? Whoever has seen me has seen the Father. How can you say, 'Show us the Father'? Do you not believe that I am in the Father and the Father is in me? The words that I say to you I do not speak on my own authority, but the Father who dwells in me does his works. Believe me that I am in the Father and the Father is in me, or*

else believe on account of the works themselves.

John 14:9-11 (ESV)

"Whoever has seen me has seen the Father." Do you need any other statement? No more parables, no more beating around the bush, and no more confusion. Jesus was not just speaking to Philip here. He was speaking to all of us. If you want to see God, look at Jesus. How does God talk? Look at how Jesus talked. How would God respond to this situation? Look at how Jesus responded. What kind of people does God pursue? Look at who Jesus pursued.

This unity of God and Jesus is the very thing that separates Christianity from every other faith. Every other monotheistic religion, even false teachings of Christianity, is teaching us what we have to do to get to God. This is why so many of us are lost and giving up in our efforts to reach a place where we can finally see God in a tangible way. What if we've been missing it all along? Although we know what we are looking for, what if we were looking in the wrong place? What if we realized that the ultimate goal was not about us going to God? The true beauty of the story is the fact that

God came to us! Jesus, God in the flesh, came and experienced everything we experience on a daily basis. What if that was part of His whole plan? If everything we experience has the potential to connect us with Jesus, everything we experience was meant to point us back to God. We are a generation begging to see more of God but failing to notice Him. God gave us a gift and exposed His ultimate plan when Jesus stepped into this world. God revealed His desire to reveal Himself.

Conclusion

There Will Be A Day

The goal of this book was to help us see that God really does want to reveal Himself to us through our faith. He does not always show up the way we expect Him to or even the way we want Him to, but He *does* show up. Adam and Eve got to experience something we all long for. They got to walk with God, talk with God, and tangibly see God. It was beautiful. There was nothing separating them from their Creator, and everything was as it was meant to be.

Unfortunately something went wrong. The reality is that God is not tangible for us today. It is not like how it was before the fall no matter how much we want it to be. Even though God is revealing Himself to us in so many different ways, life is hard, and it is so difficult for us to see Him the way we want to. We cannot deny the separation we feel. This is exactly why there is so much hurt, pain, and hatred in our world today. Although it sounds strange, I am grateful for these things. I remain grateful because these are the things that make me strive for what is coming. Jesus was God's way of coming to us for a brief time, but He did not stay for long. Before He left, however, He gave a promise of hope. He gave us something to strive for and something to look forward to. Let's look at the promise He gave in John 14.

> *"Let not your hearts be troubled. Believe in God; believe also in me. In my Father's house are many rooms. If it were not so, would I have told you that I go to prepare a place for you? And if I go and prepare a place for you, I will come again and will take you to myself, that where I am you may be also."*
>
> John 14:1-3 (ESV)

Jesus said that He went to prepare a place for us. That means today, in this moment, in your hurt, pain, and hatred, Jesus is getting everything ready for you. Although God is not physically with us, He is spiritually with us, and He is surely coming back to us. When God makes a promise, you can count on it. He says that He will come again and take us to Himself, that where He is we can be also. Jesus is joyfully telling us that there will be a day when things are back to the way they were meant to be. A time is coming when we will walk in the garden with God again. This is where our hope lies. It does not rest in where this world is headed or what happens all around us or even in the decisions other people make. Our hope is found in God's promise in John 14 that shows that God wants us and is coming to bring us back to Himself. Until that day comes, my prayer is that our eyes become open to the glory of God all around us.